# HOW TO DECORATE A DUMP

A forlorn dump waiting to be loved and made beautiful.

# HOW TO DECORATE A DUMP
## BY PHILIP ALMEIDA

A MAIN STREET PRESS BOOK

**LYLE STUART, INC. · SECAUCUS, NEW JERSEY**

First edition, 1983

Published by Lyle Stuart Inc.
120 Enterprise Avenue
Secaucus, New Jersey 07094

Published simultaneously in Canada by Musson Book Company
A division of General Publishing Co. Limited
Don Mills, Ontario

Designed by Frank Mahood

Produced by The Main Street Press

Printed in Singapore

**Library of Congress Cataloging in Publication Data**

Almeida, Philip.
   How to decorate a dump.

   "A Main Street Press book."
   Includes index.
    1. Interior decoration—Handbooks, manuals, etc.
I. Title.
NK2115.A594 1983    747    83-13609
ISBN 0-8184-0346-2

For my mother and father,

WHO TAUGHT ME HOW TO MAKE

THE MOST OF WHAT I HAVE.

# CONTENTS

# INTRODUCTION

"What a dump!"—Bette Davis in *Beyond the Forest* (1949)

THE YEAR IS 1949. Forced into still another turkey by Jack Warner, the inimitable Bette Davis is at the end of her tether—and at the end of her eighteen-year tenure at Warner Bros. This time the turkey is *Beyond the Forest*, a steamy, nostril-flaring melodrama of lust, adultery, murder, and peritonitis—the latter the price one pays, according to the Production Code, for the former. Playing slatternly Rosa Moline, in a fright wig that would do justice only to Tiny Tim, there is nothing that Davis does not do to bring unhappiness to the long-suffering Wisconsin country doctor (played by Joseph Cotton) to whom she is miserably married. In the course of ninety-seven frenziedly dramatic minutes, Davis (billed as "a twelve o'clock girl in a nine o'clock town") runs off to Chicago, commits adultery with a wealthy industrialist (David Brian), induces a miscarriage by jumping off a highway embankment, and even commits murder. And, as if that were not enough, she even gets to deliver one of the most famous lines in movie history, a line parodied to great advantage years later in Edward Albee's *Who's Afraid of Virginia Woolf*, and a line, if it is not already in Bartlett's great compendium of famous quotations, that most certainly ought to be there. "What a dump!" Davis exclaims at one point, the *wh* in "what" exploding with disdain, disgust, and a burst of cigarette smoke that all but engulfs the space she is sneering at. "What a dump!" she says. Little could she have guessed that, more than three decades later, the line would be used as the springboard to the introduction of a decorating book.

*How to Decorate a Dump* has nothing whatever to do with lust, adultery, murder, or peritonitis, but it does concern itself with dumps. And for a very good reason. More people than ever before are living in them—and paying through the nose for the privilege.

Twenty years ago or more, if a person of reasonably sound mind moved into a dump—a wreck of an apartment in an uncared-for, old building, generally in a less than fashionable part of town — he was considered a "character," a nonconformist, an "artsy-craftsy" type at best, or a down-at-the-heels dissolute bum at worst. But times have changed, and with them the typical denizen of a dump.

Today a mighty housing shortage is raging, the result not only of fewer and fewer rental apartments being constructed, but of increasing numbers of older buildings "going co-op." With rental space at a premium, rents themselves have not only skyrocketed, they've gone berserk. In New York City, for example, a one-bedroom apartment in a twenty-year-old Manhattan "luxury" building — "luxury" being real estate-ese for a boring box with paper-thin walls — will set you back anywhere from 800 to 1200 bucks a month, depending upon the size of the box and the part of town in which it's located. If you can ante up that kind of dough, what you'll get for your hard-earned money is a low-ceilinged L-shaped living room that is duplicated in ten thousand other "modern" apartments, a bedroom small enough or large enough (depending upon whether you're a pessimist or an optimist) for a king-size bed and little else, a kitchen so narrow that you burn your rear on the stove each time you attempt to open the refrigerator, and a tiny bathroom without a window and without air.

But, as the real-estate ads point out, there *are* amenities — a narrow public corridor with genuine acrylic carpeting (*something* has to cover the bare concrete flooring), a lobby with an electric fountain, a paint-by-the-numbers mural and plastic philodendron, and a sullen doorman whose palm has to be crossed with silver more frequently than a fortune-telling gypsy at Coney Island. All this luxury for only fifteen thousand a year.

Miraculously, even the most boring of these cheaply-constructed cookie-cutter apartments is occupied, and lucky the tenant who for his fifteen grand doesn't have a gaggle of hairdressers or a planeload of stewardesses sharing a studio next door, or, even worse, one of those perfumed apartments where a peephole monitors the steady flow of middle-aged men who seem to come and go at all hours of the day and night.

In the face of this modern housing phenomenon has come a new breed of urban pioneer. Not the pioneer of twenty years ago who, recognizing the architectural treasures that lay decaying in old, impoverished neighborhoods, moved into the slums and "gentrified" them. Not even less visionary people who instinctively prefer the charm of the ancient to the monotony of the modern. But a new kind of tenant for the 1980s—the person who is so comfortable with the urban environment that he can live in the thick of it without pretending that he's in a vertical suburbia.

It's not at all uncommon today to find young professionals living (and thriving) in the railroad flats of tenement houses—apartments that a generation ago would have been considered beyond the pale by any "successful" man or woman. Forced out of the "luxury" housing market, or not particularly interested in it in the first place, these people have moved into whatever urban space is available, often hobnobbing with the poor, who might very well be the neighbor to the left or right, above or below them. And they are not "gentrifiers." Their landlords are. When Mrs. Smith, who moved into her apartment in 1934, dies, her five-room railroad flat, renting for $103 per month, escalates sixfold in price. Ms. Jones, who is a junior copywriter at a midtown advertising agency and fresh out of Wellesley, considers herself lucky to be moving into Mrs. Smith's fifth-floor walkup flat—cracked walls, peeling ceilings, crooked floors, faulty plumbing, wall-to-wall roaches, and all.

This book is for the Ms., Mr., and Mrs. Joneses of the urban world—for all of you who find yourselves living in dumps without the foggiest notion of what to do with them. Its intention, as should be obvious from this introduction, is to treat an unconventional subject unconventionally. *How to Decorate a Dump* is not a "how-to" book in the usual sense. It aims to teach you how to think, how to "re-see," how to conceptualize. It intends to show you how easy it is to be your own designer. Above all, it seeks to demonstrate that living in a dump can prove to be one of the most creative trips you've ever undertaken.

So let's turn the page and begin.

Clotheslines everywhere —the hallmark of the tenement dump.

# TYPES OF DUMPS

## The Tenement Dump

IN AN EARLY SCENE of the Warner Bros. biopic *Rhapsody in Blue*, the Gershwin boys, George and Ira, have been given a piano by their fawning mother. The neighbors gather round on the sidewalk of their teeming city street to watch the crated upright piano being hoisted via block and tackle to their fifth-floor walk-up tenement apartment. It is a typical Hollywood scene of hope amidst poverty and conjures up an image of a dark and dreary tenement corridor so narrow that no large piece of furniture could possibly pass through. Today, some eighty years later, the same apartment in the same building, rents for fifty times the amount Pa Gershwin had to scrape up each month to keep the landlord happy. And the stairway corridors are probably drearier than ever. But if you're suitably adventurous, and lucky enough to find a vacancy in such a building, the space within can prove a boon to the innovative tenant. Forget for the moment the quaintness of the railroad flat—the relatively small rooms (usually five) running one into the other like the cars of a railroad train that give the layout its descriptive name. Forget the bathtub in the kitchen and the cracked walls and peeling ceilings. Forget the little crawling critters, too. Even brand-new apartments develop these once the supermarket delivers them together with the groceries. Forget all the disadvantages for the moment. What you have here is the promise of space that can be put to use to fit your needs and temperament. If you're the type who likes your space carefully defined—a room for sleeping, a room for working, a room for dining—the railroad flat can fit the bill. If you're the sort who prefers each room to offer multiple functions, then the tenement dump can be made to accommodate your needs. The great advantage of the railroad flat is that the rooms, though blocked out as clearly defined spaces, are by no means architecturally defined by function. You can make each room serve the function or functions that you want it to.

13

Tight quarters in a low-grade New York apartment house, c. 1885.

# The Small Dump

WITH ONE MAJOR EXCEPTION, small dumps are generally tiny self-contained units carved out of much larger spaces—the 19th-century town house turned into a rooming house in the 1920s and then converted to one-room apartments forty years later; the early 20th-century five-room railroad flat broken in half years later with the partitions of two small rooms removed to form one multipurpose room and the remaining half-room divided into tiny bath, tinier kitchen, and minuscule entryway; or the maids' quarters on the top floor of a posh turn-of-the-century apartment building renovated to single-occupancy dwellings sometime in the maidless postwar era. And, of course, there's that comparatively modern invention, the studio apartment, ubiquitous in today's so-called "luxury" housing. In the 1930s, when such apartments were first introduced, they were intended for suburbanites who needed a pied-à-terre in town. Today they're meant for full-time living, and, if anything, are even "smaller" than their Depression-era cousins, an illusion caused by their preposterously low ceilings. The resident of the small dump, be it old or new, has one essential problem to solve: how to allow for multiple functions in one small space.

A typical industrial loft.

# The Large Dump

AMERICA'S LOVE AFFAIR with the automobile, particularly after World War II, has led directly to the most dynamic visible characteristic of the postwar era—the removal of industry from the inner city to less populated areas and the creation of new suburbs to house the workers in plants and corporate offices that have sprung up along the interstates. One result of this contemporary phenomenon has been a revolutionary new approach to housing: the conversion of urban industrial space to living space. Artists, who require room for the exercise of their craft, as well as light, were the first to take advantage of the exciting possibilities inherent in the high ceilings, enormous windows, and gargantuan spaces of industrial buildings. Their pioneering efforts in converting barn-like lofts into combination studios and residences were frequently done in violation of existing zoning laws, but they paved the way both to liberalization of such laws and (alas) the venal realization among previously disinterested landlords that abandoned industrial spaces could easily be worth their weight in residential gold. The obvious problem facing anyone fortunate enough to find an enormous dump is how on earth to divide and organize the space.

An attic room before decorating.

# The Odd-Shaped Dump

I F ARCHITECTURE were a truly democratic art, then all rooms would be created equal. But they're not. Some are bigger than others; some are beautifully detailed, others unregenerate plain Janes; innumerable others are simply odd—odd in shape, odd in proportions, odd in atmosphere. The odd-shaped dump is immediately recognizable. If a room is higher than it is wide—if the ceiling is fourteen feet from the floor but you have to squeeze to fit a double bed between its narrow walls—if the room to normal eyes appears as if it's been tilted on its side—then you can be certain that you're in a room that's been carved out of a larger space: a town house parlor with three bays, where the window on the right or left has been partitioned by some demented landlord like a bowling alley on a listing ship. If a room is more a trapezoid than a rectangle or a square, then you very likely have a corner apartment in a building built upon an odd-shaped lot. If you have to bend in two to open your bedroom window, then you're obviously housed within the attic of a house or beneath the ornamental roof of an ancient apartment building. Don't despair. Oddness equals character, color, individuality, uniqueness, interest.

The modern urban plague—a rabbit warren of box-like boring dumps.

# The Lifeless Dump

AT OVER A GRAND per month for a one-bedroom box in a modern Gotham high-rise or a stripped-down converted brownstone, it might seem a trifle off the wall to call such luxury apartments dumps. But a dump by any other name is still a dump, so why mince words? No matter the exorbitant rent, the contemporary plaster box is sterile, boring, cold. In short, a dump. And it's not merely the cheapness of materials that can depress the spirit and keep it low—the toilet flushing on the ninth floor that is heard as a matter of course on the second, or the hollow composition doors that weigh only slightly more than the simulated bronze doorknobs. It's the sleazy architecture itself—stamped out, prefabricated, standardized: preposterously low ceilings, no moldings to separate ceilings from walls, cheap aluminum windows that pit within a year, windowless kitchens, windowless baths. In other words, an architecture that creates lifeless environments; an architecture completely without character; an architecture where, far from being "more," less is merely less. A boring dump can be made liveable, but it will take as much effort to add life and interest to it as it does to cover up the cracks in a tenement dump.

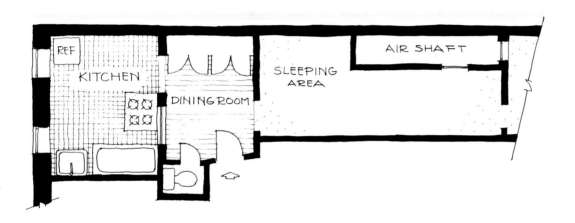

# Decorating The Tenement Dump

SINCE THIS BOOK ends with a dream—a series of "dream dumps" that illustrate the unlimited potentiality of decorating a dump—then let it begin with a dream as well—a dream come true, a true story, the story of Charles and the grungy railroad flat he moved into fifteen years ago.

When Charles, a lawyer, first moved into the turn-of-the-century tenement, his rent was $51 a month. On entering the apartment, outlined in the floor plans on the opposite page, its promise was not immediately apparent. The first room encountered was a hallway into which was built a primitive water closet. In the kitchen, to the left, was a stove, a sink, and—horrors!—a bathtub. The entry hall was separated from the kitchen by a door and a window, a window similar to those found in the other partitions between rooms to allow light and air to filter through. What Charles did, after laying out a floor plan on graph paper, was to turn his entry foyer into a separate dining room, a long-standing dream. Taking advantage of the bathtub in the kitchen, he divided the ample-sized room into a kitchen and a bath, moving the toilet from the water closet (which eventually became a coat closet by the front door) to the new windowed bathroom. To accomplish this, he had to elevate the new bathroom on a wooden platform, required to accommodate the plumbing for the toilet. Before he did any of this, he received estimates on the cost of building the dividing wall, of laying tile, installing plumbing—in short, of hiring someone to build his bathroom for him. Fifteen years ago, this cost him less than $900, but he saved considerably by buying used bathroom fixtures. To upgrade the kitchen, he bought used appliances, too. He also bought used kitchen cabinets from the 1930s, painted them, and put on new hardware.

*Opposite page:* Floor plan of a tenement railroad flat, before and after renovation.

Once the kitchen and bath were complete, Charles concentrated on creating a strong, clean background for his apartment. Over the years, he continually replastered the cracked, broken walls, carefully repainted them, and kept replacing his furniture and paying a bit more for something better. Eventually, he had a place furnished in good pieces against walls that were now as straight and smooth as the walls in "fancy" buildings. He had created backgrounds that were strong—a gallery for his furniture.

Even though Charles had a double bed, he took advantage of the walk-through plan of the railroad flat to play down the odd effect of a bedroom immediately next to the dining room. Guests passing through the bedroom on the way to the living room generally viewed it as a sitting room, the bed doing double duty as a sofa when covered. (In railroad flats, it's a good idea to set up the bedroom as a sitting room, since every room is more or less visible.) True, Charles could have used the large windowed parlor at the far end of the apartment as a bedroom instead of as a living room, thereby gaining complete privacy. But he preferred a larger space in which to entertain. Besides, the parlor room fronted on a busy city street and he found an inner room more restful for sleeping.

Charles built a closet around the tenement air shaft, thereby solving his bedroom storage problems and hiding the ugly window that looks out at a brick wall only a few feet away. He covered up the window to the air shaft in the adjoining room by building shelves. Tenement dumps, like any other city apartments, can be notoriously hot in the humid summer months, so Charles eased his ventilation/cooling problems by installing air conditioners in a living room window and in the sitting room closet that was fitted with louvered doors.

When Charles's building finally "went co-op," he bought his apartment at the insider's price of $35,000. He eventually sold it for $80,000—a profit of well over 100 percent, including the total amount spent improving the once-crummy dump. He not only doubled his money, but he had fifteen years of living with a low rent. Naturally, your rent won't exactly be as low as his, but you can realize a similar profit when your dump goes co-op. And it will.

Charles's story is a dream come true. It exemplifies that dump-dwellers are a tribe of special people, resourceful people, clever people. Like many people who move into such apartments, he started out by collecting discarded furniture from the streets. Charles continually sold what he had, turning his junk into money, and then "traded up." The profit that he made allowed him to go to flea markets, thrift shops, and keep going. Eventually, his apartment was completely furnished in Art Deco pieces, which he loved in particular, but when Deco lost its appeal to him, he thought it was time for a change. Once again, he traded up. By the time he sold his apartment, it was furnished in approximately $30,000 worth of 18th-century English antiques and paintings—all in the same railroad flat where he had begun with virtually nothing. Starting with a dump with a bathtub in the kitchen, Charles wound up with an $80,000 cooperative apartment. This is the kind of real-estate story that gives one goose bumps. But it's true—and it can happen to you.

The tenement dump illustrated in color on the following two pages is furnished entirely with objects purchased inexpensively from thrift shops or found on the street. The apartment, in a converted rooming house built in the last century, was originally one room, but the tenant, a student of design, rented a vacant apartment next door and joined the two by breaking through the walls and hanging a pair of French doors. The illustrations that follow show what can be done with a can of paint, a minimal budget, a fertile imagination, some basic sewing skills, and a great deal of elbow grease.

*Opposite page*: An apartment in a former rooming house. The walls beyond the French doors were in such bad shape that the plaster was completely removed to expose the handsome brick. The pillows, originally bed pillows, were purchased for a song from a hotel going out of business and were covered with fabric remnants. The striped silk pillow was found on the street and dry-cleaned to good effect. The chairs—simple rattan seating found at a thrift shop—were padded with several of the hotel pillows and covered with suede skins given the designer by a friend. (The same effect, of course, can be had by using any heavy fabric.) The sofa is a discarded single bed, completely covered by hand with fabric. The terra-cotta paint more than holds its own as an alternative to costly wallpaper, and the plants on the window sill not only double for expensive draperies, but help to give the space its roomy, open feeling. *Left*: The cracked walls of the bedroom are hidden by fabric hung on traverse rods. The old-fashioned portière and matching bedspread are made of draperies found in a thrift shop. The monumental headboard is an imaginative use of two dresser mirrors of the 1920s piled one upon the other. Like the paper umbrella, hung from wires as a ceiling fixture, the mirrors were found in a second-hand store. The covered hotel pillows finish off the room, the key ingredients of which are imagination and skill with a needle and thread. (All of these inexpensive, yet attractive items, should be looked upon as "stepping stones"—that is, objects to be used until you can afford to "trade up.")

With ceilings, walls, and floor painted with as many as nine coats of dazzling white paint to make them virtually invisible, this dramatic tenement apartment has been transformed into a "mini-loft"—a space meant to serve as background for its furnishings, so highlighted that they seem to shine as works of art.

# Decorating the Small Dump

JIM BRINKLEY is a young graphic designer with a keen dramatic sensibility, a limited budget, and a knack for convincing a coterie of gifted friends to contribute to the design of his unusually stark and architectural apartment. This collaborative effort, with Jim serving as coordinator, overseer, and chief laborer, is pictured on the opposite page. Its fundamental aim, admirably achieved, was to turn a tiny one-room apartment into a "mini-loft," to use the small space he occupies and make it function as a gallery that would turn his furniture into art objects. To achieve this aim meant (among other things) obliterating everything he did not want to be seen by painting it a brilliant white, including ceiling, walls, and the complete expanse of floor. The walls, for example, are covered with *nine* coats of white paint, giving them a textured appearance. This juxtaposition of texture upon texture takes its cue from the sculptor Louise Nevelson. Where she takes found objects and paints them, Jim has taken a "found object"—his tiny one-room dump—and painted it to make it appear to be a work of art.

Originally a laborer's flat in a tenement built in the 19th century for longshoremen working on the New York City docks, the apartment had walls that were a veritable patchwork of bumps. gouges, and cracks and a useless dividing wall between areas of the room with a windowed pass-through that had functioned as a previous tenant's bar. Jim Brinkley removed this obstruction, thus opening up the space, and conceived the idea of a sculptured wall that would become the dramatic highlight of his gallery "mini-loft." Translating his idea into actuality required the talents of Dane Goodman, a conceptual artist who had acquired sound technical experience in converting a large loft for his wife and himself. With Jim serving as co-constructor, the drywall sculpture cost less than $500 to erect and functions only incidentally as a room divider, separating the kitchen area from the rest of the apartment. Since the wall's primary purpose is purely sculptural, it's no exaggeration to say that, in this particular case, function follows form.

Installing new louvered doors on a preexisting closet, Jim constructed a cabinet opposite the closet that provided additional storage space and defined a small but needed dressing area. This cabinet also functions as an "arm" of the sofa, which doubles as a bed at night once the pillows are removed. The hand-painted bed covering was created, after ascertaining Brinkley's needs, by Corbett Reynolds, a fabric and wallpaper designer. The lighting in the apartment is both casual and suitably dramatic: theatrical lights are suspended from the ceiling and are plugged into outlets placed where wall sconces used to be.

Shelves over the stove hold a collection of 1930s refrigerator ware and provide a touch of brilliant color. Like the sculptured wall and the textured bed fabric, even the shelves are a collaborative effort. Suggested by Jim Brinkley, they were designed by the author of this book.

## Kitchens and Bathrooms

One of the problems in decorating a small dump—or any dump, for that matter—is what on earth to do with kitchens, more often than not ridiculously small, that not only have seen better days, but which seem incorrigibly hopeless by the cold light of morn. Unless you're one of the few who has not been caught up in America's love affair with gourmet cooking, or unless plain old economic necessity hasn't dictated that you're going to have to eat in most of the workaday week, then the kitchen is almost sure to prove one of the most actively lived-in areas of your space. And a dismal kitchen can be not only a royal pain in the neck, but a primary source of depression in your life. Aside from the pathetically antiquated fixtures and appliances that are the lot of almost every dumpy kitchen, the most frequently encountered problems are: (1) kitchens that are too small, allowing only a bare minimum of storage space; (2) kitchens that are too large, or so badly arranged that space is almost criminally wasted; and (3) kitchens that are

## Decorating the Small Dump

*Left*: A tenement kitchen before the invasion of imagination and a paint brush. *Right*: The same kitchen, after.

so far gone that they require complete replacement and a major outlay of cash. If you find yourself with problem 3, then you need a bank and not this book. One solution to problem 2 – dividing the space into more useful components – has already been suggested in the discussion of the floor plans on page 18. Which leaves us with the problems of the too-small, dumpy kitchen: the most usual problem of them all.

When interior designer Richard Des Jardins moved into an antiquated West Side dump, the kitchen that he found (illustrated above, at left) was a typical disaster. It was long and narrow, the walls cracked and grungy, the sink chipped and much too shallow to hold more than a dish or two, and the single storage area and work space a wooden board above the sink. The room's one and only blessing was its generously proportioned window, a harbinger of light in the otherwise unprepossessing kitchen.

The transformation wrought by Des Jardins is apparent in the accompanying photograph to the right. And it took not much more than a bucket of paint to create his most interesting effect. To begin with, the appliances were replaced with more useful fixtures bought secondhand. (With most Americans conventionally dazzled by the new, discarded kitchen sinks and stoves can be purchased used for very little money.) The secondhand sink provided a small work area and badly needed storage space below. The dishwasher, a hand-me-down donated by a friend, added additional counter space. The walls, originally cracked and peeling, were patched and painted white to the level of the wooden cabinet, purchased inexpensively at an unpainted furniture emporium. With the appliances of necessity white, the lower walls were kept the same color to de-emphasize the secondhand fixtures. The upper walls and the ceiling were painted a dark blue, which not only created the illusion of the ceiling being lower than it really is in the exceptionally narrow room, but disguised the uneven, bumpy walls so typical of tenement dwellings. The floor was painted white, with a practical and inexpensive sisal mat placed upon it for comfort while preparing meals. The white-porcelain ceiling fixture, much like the fixtures over old-fashioned billiard tables, was found in a junk shop for a couple of dollars. It focuses light on the white portions of the kitchen, deflecting close examination of the uneven and frequently patched tenement ceiling. The window remains the focal point of the room. A hanging plant softens its architectural lines and provides a sense of privacy without the need for more expensive and obfuscating window treatments. The total cost of transforming this room to a delightful, functional kitchen is less than $300, provided that you do the work yourself, of course.

---

Through the simple use of hardware, paint, and glass, the handsome kitchen on the opposite page was transformed from the ugly room it used to be. Designers Nicholas Politis and Richard Des Jardins were asked to renovate a kitchen that had been decorated with many of the garish excrescenses of the 1950s.

**Decorating
the Small
Dump**

These inexpensive and
attractive cabinets were
once ponderous and
ugly. An easy method of
upgrading ungainly
cabinets without replac-
ing them is discussed in
the accompanying text.

The cabinets in particular bore the hallmarks of the period's shoddy design and poor workmanship. Pressed-wood moldings surrounded them to give the impression of Mediterranean "richness," and the doors were faced with bottle-green plexiglas in a bull's-eye pattern that wobbled and trembled every time the cabinets were opened. The designers removed the ornate moldings and replaced the plexiglas with glass with wire netting running through it, creating a pleasant linear effect. This effect they repeated by using a wallpaper with a similar pattern beneath the hanging cabinets. By changing the hardware, painting the walls (in this case gray), and adding a few well-chosen accessories, an eyesore was rendered beautiful.

With a somewhat different problem to solve — she was redesigning her tiny kitchen from scratch — image consultant Lillian Cortez looked through interior design magazines to find a kitchen that would suit her aesthetic and functional needs. She simply scaled down what she found to the dimensions of her room, researched the sources for the appliances she wanted as a gourmet cook, and mapped out the entire project on graph paper. After getting estimates for the job from three contractors, she proceeded to do the work herself for less than half the price of the lowest bid. The result is pictured on the opposite page. Yes, she had help with the plumbing and electrical work, but the rest she did alone, including the ingenious notion of incorporating the shelving tracks within the grouting of the tiles, thus hiding the most unattractive aspect of this convenient store-bought shelving. The shelves themselves are of wire-reinforced glass. Tiled throughout, the kitchen is easy to maintain and never requires painting.

A maintenance-free kitchen designed and executed by an intrepid do-it-yourselfer at less than half the cost of the lowest contractor's bid.

*Left*; A bathroom in an urban tenement before renovation. *Opposite page:* The same bathroom, after.

If the kitchen of an unconverted dump presents a drove of problems, then the bathroom, as a rule, is even worse. Carved from a closet or a corner of a room after modern sanitary laws brought an end to water closets shared by neighbors on a common floor, the typically ramshackle tenement john is small, grim, cold, and bare—undoubtedly the most forbidding room in the entire dump. But it lends itself to solutions that are simple, spare, and relatively inexpensive if cool heads, sound judgment, and good design sense prevail.

The bathroom that architectural designer Leonard Braunschweiger inherited when he moved into his New York City dump was anything but uncommon. A bathtub dominated the monk-sized cell, pic-

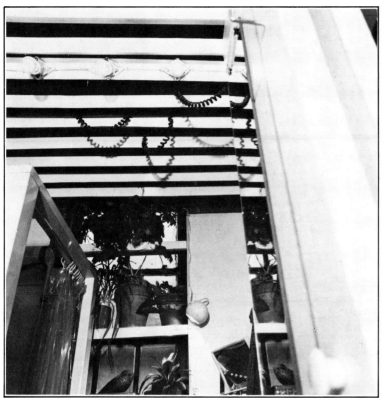 

tured above. The only other fixture was the w.c. Since there was no bathroom sink, such standard exercises as shaving and washing one's hands were accomplished in the kitchen sink following the demise of the once ubiquitous practice of using a marble-topped washstand and china pitcher and bowl.

By removing the ancient bathtub and replacing it with a stall shower, the designer gained valuable space both for storage shelves and for a corner sink. And by installing wooden boards across the length of the ceiling, he simultaneously created the illusion of lowering the ceiling (and improving the proportions of the tiny room) and provided the place to mount his ingeniously simple lights. The resulting room is spare, functional, and, above all, honest in its no-nonsense masculinity.

If you've moved into a dump with a bathroom previously tiled, then you've probably inherited a blessing that is simultaneously a curse. If the tile is in reasonably good shape, you'll naturally want to keep it in place since the replacement cost might prove enough to break your meager bank account. But you'll be forced to live with a color combination of the past that is either adaptable like simple black and white, or quaintly dated like the maroon and gray favored in the 1930s. It's generally unwise to try to cover over tile with paint. Since most bathrooms were originally only partially tiled, it's far better to learn to live with the color of the tile, no matter how *de trop*, by selecting a corresponding or complementary color for either painting or papering the walls and ceiling. It's a challenge to be sure, but why rebuild your landlord's property unless it's absolutely necessary?

In a sense, you have far greater decorating options if you're renovating a really cruddy untiled dump. The bathroom pictured on the opposite page is a perfect case in point. Created by interior designer Juan Montoya, the long and narrow tenement room is a marvel of innovative, inexpensive, clean design. Of the three bathroom fixtures, only the toilet is a replacement. The vintage World War I enamel sink and tub and the nickel shower-curtain rod have been retained. What appears to be a vast expanse of dazzling white tile is actually imitation tile, the kind available in home supply and hardware stores on strips of masonite. The tile completely hides the bumpy and uneven tenement walls and ceiling and provides attractive storage space when laid around the ancient sink and a bank of exposed heating and plumbing pipes. A needed touch of color is supplied by the stacks of towels and the enamel-painted tub.

*Opposite page:*
A tenement bathroom innovatively and inexpensively renewed—without replacing most of the original fixtures.

When you're fortunate enough to own your own loft, you are free to plan the proportions of your rooms as you see fit. Photographer Peter M. Fine has cut his costs considerably by installing standard bathroom fixtures, but he has wisely invested his savings in rich redwood shelving, floors, and furnishings. Built upon a platform to provide the space for pipes where no plumbing had previously existed, the bathroom cheerfully suggests the great outdoors within an indoor urban setting—an aim accomplished by the many plants, the deep-grained patina of native western redwood, and the brilliant lighting under lucite panels meant to simulate a skylight where none actually exists. The floor is laid in sections to provide easy access to the pipes below.

# Decorating the Large Dump

WITH THE EXCEPTION of lofts in abandoned industrial buildings, large dumps hardly exist at all. Large apartments are either generally well maintained in better buildings or they are subdivided into smaller flats so that landlords can increase the profit on their investments. The large apartment in an antiquated building has gone the way of the dodo bird, and it looks as if the loft at a halfway affordable purchase price is rapidly headed down a similar road to ultimate extinction.

There was a time, of course, and in the recent past, when artists were among the very first to realize the unlimited potential of the space within decaying industrial sites. Like the pioneers they were, painters and sculptors, photographers and others in need of light and space began to settle in—often in advance of zoning regulations that permitted them the luxury of attempting the impossible. These first attempts at imposing order on a large unmanageable space often resembled little more than hastily built masses of lumber, crudely dividing spaces helter-skelter and at random. But the basic problem of the loft had already been convincingly exposed: how to arrive at a functional and practical layout that divided the space into carefully defined areas.

The lot of pioneers is not a happy one, and as word spread of the architectural possibilities of industrial lofts, the world of real estate quickly moved in to profit from what was once considered a hopeless cause. With lofts now selling for at least as much as cooperative apartments in the better urban neighborhoods, and with the cost of conversion easily running into additional tens of thousands of dollars, let's not kid ourselves: you don't need a book to tell you what to do, you need the help of a professional designer and a bank loan. Still, it doesn't hurt to dream, so turn the page.

If the greatest problem of living and working in a loft is the division of space, then the designer of the loft illustrated above and on the opposite page has solved the problem admirably and elegantly. In one case, furniture alone defines the function of the space. The table, exquisitely laid, suggests a formal dining room for a black-tie sit-down dinner. Less elaborately set, it could function as a buffet at a large informal party. And with the table set aside, the open space could function as most anything—say, with an exercise mat spread out to stay in shape, or a stationary bicycle moved in place for the same purpose. With a dividing wall erected beneath a structural beam and intersected by a cutout circle and an Art Deco arch, the sitting area is meticulously defined. The shelf built out from the windows and hung with pleated draperies hides ugly radiators without cutting off their heat—an excellent solution to a problem common in both lofts and smaller spaces.

The extreme height of
this disproportionately
narrow room is visually
lowered by the raised
platform at one end and
by the horizontality of
the monumental
mantel, the banquette,
and the curtains that do
not rise to the full
height of the windows.

# Decorating the Odd-Shaped Dump

DUMPS COME in all shapes and sizes, but the most frequently encountered odd-shaped spaces are rooms that are disproportionately higher than they are wide. Although this situation usually ensues when a large room has been carved out into smaller units, some tall and narrow rooms were originally built that way at a time when opulence was the watchword in town houses built on narrow city lots. Two solutions to the problem of the ill-proportioned room are illustrated in these pages. Another common problem—the attic room—is pictured and discussed on page 54.

To break up the extreme verticality of the high-ceilinged room shown on the opposite page, designer Juan Montoya constructed a platform across the narrow width at the window end. Serving as a dining area, the raised platform not only seems to lower the extreme height of the room, but appears to widen it as well. This effect is underscored by the strategic placement of a sofa, matched to the height of the platform, that seemingly extends the platform forward and visually enhances its horizontal line.

The small fireplace opening has deliberately been given a monumental mantel. Designed to resemble massive blocks of granite arranged in a pleasing architectural configuration, the mantel and its illusion of sheer weight contrive with the platform to lower the ceiling and widen the room. The banquette at the left, by being intentionally narrow, de-emphasizes the extreme length of the room and contributes to the illusion of its being wider than it actually is.

The handsome window treatment, incidentally, is a brilliant solution to a common urban problem: the view is an abomination that would detract from the eloquence of the room if freely seen. By painting the windows a vibrantly cheerful green and by placing sheer curtains over them to obscure the view, the designer chose not to play down the windows but to emphasize their architectural importance. Once

## Decorating the Odd-Shaped Dump

If a room is long and narrow, the solution is often simple: build up! Here a child's room illustrates the principle. A group of lacquered furniture pieces in graduated sizes, with wooden boxes as risers, forms a staircase to a sleeping loft. The effect is playful, imaginative, practical—a room that any child would want to live in and play in.

again, the curtains do not rise the full height of the windows in order to stress the horizontality of the room and not its verticality. In brightening the windows with color and in hazing over the view, the total window treatment can be likened to photographing an old actress through gauze.

---

The child's room pictured on the opposite page illustrates another fundamental solution to the long and narrow room: *build up!* A happy alternative to raised platforms, these heavily lacquered boxes are stacked up to form a staircase to a sleeping loft. And, of course, the boxes—really wooden shelves of graduated sizes—serve another function as well by providing ample storage space for toys and games. One unit, directly underneath the loft, serves as a convenient study desk.

In creating an atmosphere of playful fantasy, the design is very clever—and inexpensive to bring off. The desk and shelving units can be easily obtained at any unpainted-furniture store, and the boxes, functioning as risers, are readily purchasable or just as simply made.

A day bed placed at the window end of the room would allow the loft to be used exclusively as a play area, a sort-of "tree house" in an urban room, or the loft could be used to accommodate a child's overnight guest. By building up, the room can easily house two children in a family. Designed with flair and imagination, this ingenious child's bedroom is both practical and easy on the family budget.

The usual depressing view from a ground-floor apartment in a tenement or a converted town house is a row of garbage cans seen through prison-like security bars *(left)*. Since a space of several feet usually separates the window from a retaining wall before the sidewalk, this space can be utilized to good effect by building an outdoor window box holding plants and shrubs or even small trees *(right)*. The greenery not only hides the garbage cans, but allows the eye to travel past the iron bars, thus obscuring them. Outdoor lighting can enhance the garden view at night. A similar treatment can considerably brighten air shaft windows.

# Dealing with Outside Spaces

IN RECENT TIMES living space has become relatively limited in size. Whether you reside in a so-called "luxury" building or in a renovated tenement, your space has been badly constricted. The excessive cost of both building anew and of renovation has forced landlords to decrease the area of space available to tenants. Particularly in renovated buildings, what was once a residence for a single family is now divided into as many as ten studio apartments. With actual living space becoming smaller year by year, the importance of space beyond your immediate four walls is becoming proportionally greater.

The small terrace, the pleasant view, or even the brick wall you face, or perhaps your front door and the public hallway beyond should all be thought of as extensions of your living space. If you see it often, or even sense its presence, then you must consider it an integral part of your dwelling.

If you are fortunate enough to have an interesting view, then arrange your activities within your space to take advantage of that view. If you spend a great deal of time working at a desk, for instance, try to place the desk so that you may look out upon the view, or to the side, or whatever way is most comfortable to catch the sunset or the skyline set beyond. If the primary use of the room is for seating guests in conversation, then arrange the sitting area so that most people can take advantage of the view. In this case, your window treatment should maximize the space beyond by obscuring it as little as possible. Whatever covering is used should be pushed back when you want the view exposed. The window in a room with a view is very important: once designed, a room remains visually the same; but a view changes with the light of day, with the seasons of the year.

Urban gardens are generally long and narrow. When the occupants of three brownstone buildings joined forces collectively to beautify their backyard gardens, they used surplus sewer covers, laid in circles and semicircles, to give the effect of enhanced horizontality. The gardens were planted in pachysandra, a vigorous ground cover valued for its ability to thrive in dense shade. Shown here are the gardens while work was in progress and a detail of the finished project.

"Window landscaping" can range from a simple window box to whatever flights of fancy your imagination and your budget will allow. Here a latticework box, built to cover the outside of an exterior window or an interior air shaft, obscures a terrible view and holds plants that bring a sense of the outdoors within. The top of the latticework box should be kept open to allow as much light as possible to nourish the plants. The effect is that of a large terrarium and negates the need for any additional window treatment.

More frequently than not, rows of tenements or converted town houses on parallel streets will look back to back upon an open space trying very hard to be a garden. Sometimes, a lone ginkgo tree, with the fortitude of all eternity, provides a welcome bit of green between the dangling maze of clotheslines overhead. The trouble with such urban backyard gardens, as anyone who has lived with one can tell, is that they are the receptacles for anything and everything thrown from adjacent windows, instant garbage dumps as it were. But human nature, to say the least, is certainly peculiar. Most people have an innate respect for the beautiful. Crowded, anti-human urban streets are certain magnets for discarded junk, whereas fewer people dare to litter well-maintained and cared-for open spaces.

The gardens illustrated on page 46 represent a communal attempt by occupants of three contiguous brownstone residences in Brooklyn, New York, to beautify and unify the garden areas behind their houses. Each plot is long and narrow, measuring 45 by 18 feet. To create a unified effect when viewed from the windows above, the landscape architect Halsted Welles planned a series of circular shapes, some running across the borders of two contiguous gardens at once, that not only effected a unity of form, but also seemed to widen the plots by visually linking them together horizontally. The round objects, planted with a ground cover of pachysandra, which thrives abundantly in shade, are surplus sewer covers. Most of the labor was done by the tenants themselves, thus limiting their costs to materials and a consulting fee for the talented designer. Although this plan was conceived as a group venture, it can be applied as well to a single backyard garden space. The circular effect will distract the eye from the long and narrow plot that is most common in urban gardens.

---

If you don't have a garden of your own, or if your windows don't look down upon one, then there is much that you can do to bring a sense of the outdoors within the confines of your interior space. Learn to experiment with what I choose to call "window landscaping." If you have a terrible view, or if your window looks out on a barren brick wall, or if you want to neutralize the ugliness of an air shaft, then your window landscape can consist of something as simple as a window box or rise to whatever flights of fancy your imagination and your pocketbook will allow. An example of a suitable ground-floor window treatment is illustrated on page 44. Another treatment is shown on page 47.

The focal point of a modern box-like apartment—a sterile, lifeless dump—is often a narrow balcony that substantially increases your rent, decreases the size of your inner space, and is moreover infrequently used. There is no way to ignore it and its usually ugly railing and the green plastic divider or concrete wall that separates it from your neighbor's balcony on the other side. Like it or not, it's an extension of your room, and, unless you keep your curtains permanently drawn, all eyes will focus on it. One solution to this common problem is illustrated on the opposite page.

The balcony of a modern low-ceilinged apartment can easily become one of the dumpiest of spaces, a storage area for a broken bicycle or a place to stash the family dog. Rather than having a clutter of folding chairs and a collection of half-dead, sunburned plants, why not actually *design* the space? A length of canvas can obscure the ugly railing and, together with the canvas side curtain, keep down troublesome gusts of air. The curtain can provide a modicum of privacy from nosy neighbors. A narrow wooden banquette provides seating and is easily washable once the urban soot begins to take its toll. If you're not much of a gardener, a single potted tree will do. If the city air eventually kills it, it can be easily replaced.

**Decorating the Lifeless Dump**

A modern apartment tower. For thirty years these boring boxes piled atop boxes and faced with sterile white or red hospital brick have dominated the contemporary housing market. But their cold, monotonous interiors are far from hopeless, and it doesn't take too much imagination to fight ice with the fire of good design.

# Decorating the Lifeless Dump

WHAT CAN BE DONE to warm up a cold dump?

Essentially, the typical L-shaped living room/dining room area layout of a sterile, modern apartment complex squats under depressingly low ceilings and is hemmed in by paper-thin walls that form completely unbroken lines and are unadorned with moldings of any kind at all. The furnishings, in keeping with the characterless surroundings, frequently affect the "Haitian cotton" look so commonly found today in popular-priced furniture stores.

How is one to cope with such dispiriting boredom without making prohibitively expensive architectural alterations? The solution is more simple than you'd think. Wonders can be wrought by fighting ice with fire, by warming up the climate with color and other inexpensive stratagems of good design.

A good example of what can be done to dissipate the chill of cookie-cutter architecture is illustrated on the following page. Here interior designer David Hecht uses palm trees in wicker baskets, a wicker chaise, pastel colors, and light—lots of light—filtering linearly through Venetian blinds to suggest spring weather in the tropics, to impose the sense of outdoor space indoors, to hint at everything warm and pleasant that a garden on an island paradise can be. The effect is sunny, cheerful, warm. The color and the furnishings distract the eye, not from the room itself, but from the *atmosphere* of the modern room. It is no longer cold. The temperature of the interior has risen quite substantially. And nothing has been permanently installed. Everything, including the wicker stork, can be taken with you when you move.

Pastel colors, wicker furnishings, and natural light combine to transform the chilly atmosphere of this modern apartment into a pleasant ambience of considerable charm and warmth.

# Sizing-Up Your Dump

Having seen the basic types of dumps available in today's housing market, and a few examples of what can be done to turn these dumps into imaginative, comfortable living spaces, it's now time to take stock before moving on to some of the basic principles of design that you'll be encountering when it comes time to decorate your own dump.

There are at least three occasions when you will find yourself slowing down and stopping what you're doing in order to cast a cold and probing eye on your space—three occasions when you will be sizing-up your dump. The first will be when the landlord, or his agent, or the super's wife, or the straggly-haired, pot-smoking present tenant shows it to you for the first time—the time when, embarrassed by walking past other people's unmade beds and nosing through their closets, you'll have to decide whether or not you're going to take the plunge and sign a lease. The second time will occur after you've signed the lease, after you've hit the piggy bank again to come up with the standard month's rent plus a month's security, and, now, standing within the empty, paint-peeling wreck of a space, with palms sweaty and knees wobbly, and fighting off that sinking feeling that says, "Oh, God, I'm in over my head," you martial up your strength, renew the color in your face and your enthusiasm, and say, "O.K., what am I going to do with this dump to make it wonderful?" The third time will occur months, or even years, later, when having made the space comfortable and livable you realize that a design is never "finished," that a space is always evolving, forever in a state of "becoming," and that there are all sorts of things that you're going to want to do to improve on what you already have.

These three occasions that find you alone in contemplation within the four walls of your dump require concentration, deliberate consideration, thoughtful analysis. You must walk through the space, asking yourself fundamental questions about yourself, about your lifestyle, about your very personality.

Are you in the habit of giving sit-down dinners for twelve? Will this be possible in the confined space of this particular dump? Does your job require much work at home? Where will this be done? Are you a gourmet cook? How will you bring this off in a kitchen taller than your Cuisinart, but narrower than Julia Child? How much of your existing furniture will you hold on to? Where will it be placed? If you know yourself, you'll have dozens, scores, of similar questions. And you'll have to answer all of them eventually.

Of these three occasions, the last two can be attacked at leisure. The first—making the fateful decision about marrying yourself to an albatross of a wreck, a decision that should be contemplated with your mind working on all cylinders—is less a matter of leisure than it is owning a good pair of running shoes. The housing situation being what it is nowadays, finding a vacant place is bad enough, but getting to it before it's taken is even worse. Let's put it this way: It's pretty hard to make a leisurely, considered judgment if five or six other potential tenants, each dying to take the place sight-unseen, are yapping and nipping at your heels.

---

*Opposite page:*
After sizing-up their attic space, the owners of a rural country house immediately recognized that the tiny room beneath the eaves could not accommodate an adult of average height unless he ran the risk of becoming permanently hunched. Working on a very limited budget, designers Nicholas Politis and Richard Des Jardins transformed the space into a charming child's room, building into their design the possibility of changes as the child grows up. With its heavy-textured walls lightened with white paint to make it seem less confining, the room is cheerful, colorful, kid-like. The low shelf across the wall serves not only as a desk, but as a place for storage, the flea-market suitcases being used for the storage of the child's personal possessions (comic books and the like) that would otherwise sit out and clutter up the small room. Everything is scaled down to the child's size. With the addition of inexpensive sheets, lamps, comforters, and an area rug, the room is brought alive. And the total affect is achieved, essentially, with color.

Good design stems in part from knowing oneself, from being aware of the essential patterns of one's life. That his work is a dominant factor of his life is apparent from the multipurpose room that was once the studio of interior designer Juan Montoya. Not quite an office and not quite a traditional dwelling, the design works nonetheless as a successful realization of the designer's needs.

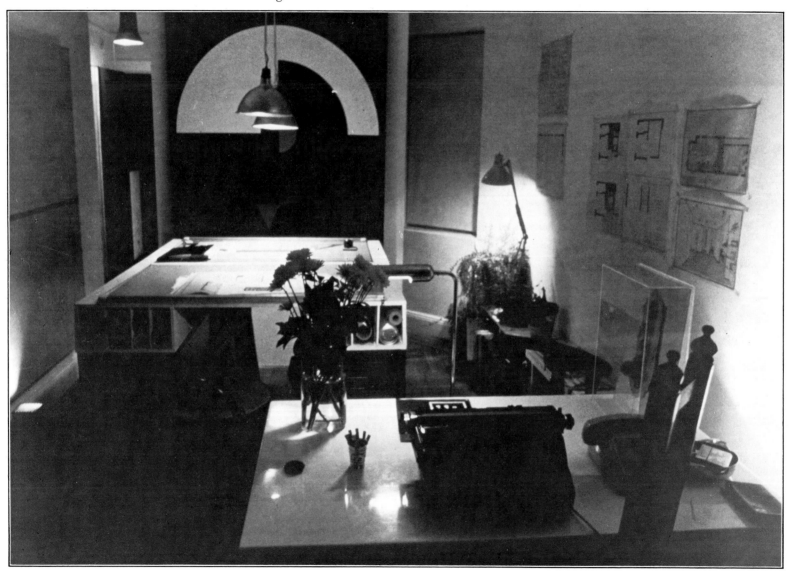

# SOME PRINCIPLES OF DESIGN

FREUD I'M NOT, but I don't have to have a degree in psychiatry or smoke a cigar to tell you a couple of things about the intimate relationship between you and design. Why should you be interested in design? Because your environment can effect you without your really being aware of it, that's why. How many years, for example, have you spent sitting at a desk with your face to the wall and your back to the room without even once thinking about moving the desk so that it "floats" in the middle of the room and allows you to look in? Try moving it and see how much better you feel, almost immediately. There are, of course, all sorts of psychological factors in your life, and your environment—where you live—is most definitely one of them. A major one. Think of it this way: You spend a great deal of time where you live. And it should be an "escape," a refuge, from the outside world—not merely from the physical elements, the snow, the rain, the wind, but an escape from outside pressures, a place where you really want to be. Even if it's a dump, it's probably the only place in your private world where you can exercise almost total control. You can add your mark to your office or place of work—a photograph here, a flowerpot there—but it really isn't yours; you're simply imposing yourself on someone else's space. But at home, wherever it may be, no one can tell you what to do. Except, perhaps, the people you live with. And that's another story.

O.K. So you've just signed the lease for your dump. What next? Just sit yourself down and start thinking logically about how to design it, since, when you're designing a home, or an apartment, or a single room, or anything, the two most important things to govern your thoughts are logic and order. You are going to have to learn how to *re-see* the ritual of your daily life, and you're going to have to learn to *ask yourself questions*. In short, you're going to treat yourself as if you were a designer dealing with yourself as a client. Since designers ask their clients many, many questions, you're going to ask yourself a battery of questions—and you're going to get into the habit of making lists.

57

The way you live your daily life now is essentially the way you'll continue to live it in your new quarters. So turn a keen eye on the events in your life as you're living it. Observe the way you live, and if there are bumpy spots, awkward setups, then you're going to do your damnedest to change them, eventually. In the same way that you walked through your space when you considered the major step of signing your lease, you should walk yourself through your life in making a series of observations about it. Analyze it. See if it makes sense. Jot down everything you do in your daily life from the minute you get up until the moment you go to bed at night. Think in terms of an average, routine day. And when you're through with that, think of how you entertain—from where you prepare the food to where you seat your guests. Then you're going to compile still further lists. Make a list of all the functions that you partake in within your space, all of the things that are "going on" within the confines of your four walls.

After you've done this, make still another list of the things you think you're going to need in your dump, from such furnishings as tables and chairs to the ashtrays if you smoke. *Do not worry about money at this point.* Make these lists without any thought of budget. After all, you're thinking of *the ideal*—and money, to say the least, only hinders what you really *want* to do. Naturally, once you've written all this down, you're going to start to eliminate many things, things you can't afford or things that are simply unnecessary once you start thinking about them. And, of course, there'll be a series of substitutions—the objects that will be temporarily substituted for the things you *really* want, until the day comes along when you can better afford them. While you're considering the things you ideally want, make certain that you know what it is you expect in a piece of furniture. It can't be comfortable, cheap, just so high, fit exactly there, and be a hundred other things. You have to decide which of these requirements is most important. In any living space, but especially in a dump, you have to learn to compromise. You're going to have to sacrifice some of the functions you might want your place to serve; and you're going to have to compromise on some of the psychological fulfillment you expect, as well.

In short, you have to learn to be reasonable. And it's much easier to be reasonable with yourself as designer than if you were an actual client dealing with an actual designer, where you'd probably be fool enough to expect the moon for your sixpence. When you're planning things on your own, however, you recognize all the more reasonably the limits of your space. There's simply no way that you can fool yourself into thinking that your preposterously tiny kitchen is going to be able to accommodate eighteen people for a sit-down dinner.

Have no fear in setting down your ideal plan once you understand that there are different stages to completing a design. You can have a long-range future plan, a plan of what the entire space is going to look like, but you obviously have to get the basics done first. Realize that your money is not going to be spent all at once—another reason for ignoring at the outset the total cost of the elements in your dream dump. Realize, too, that your time and effort are not going to be expended all at once. If you have this long-range plan, steel yourself to the reality that it is going to be a long haul, that it is going to take you a period of time to accomplish what you are setting out to do. Start with basics. The rest will eventually take care of itself over a period of time.

But you still have to set schedules and time limits. If not, you could go on forever in realizing your design. Don't get bogged down for weeks in deciding on a color scheme, for example. Make a decision and live with it. Your motto should be: Think, yes, but don't get bogged down. DO IT. If you're going to make a change in the way you live, make it quickly, otherwise you may never make it at all. DO IT. And then, gradually, you can add to your design. You can change and grow from your initial decision.

On the other hand, don't be one of those people whose places look as if they are constantly under construction—like a permanently unfinished airport. There's no reason to live in a total mess. By all means, go ahead and paint the entire place if you're not ready for the renovations you foresee in the future. If you plan on breaking through a wall to construct a new doorway, don't put off painting the dump in order to wait a year and a half before undergoing construction. If you can't afford the doorway work at first, then paint first, break through later, and touch up. Why live in a total disaster area waiting for tomorrow?

There are three basic stages of design—planning, doing, and the extras. *Planning* is talked about extensively in the chapters that follow. *Doing* is either doing things yourself or finding people to do them.

Although it's easy to look in the yellow pages for a contractor, that's not exactly what I have in mind by the term "doing." I'm talking about researching, about researching sources of supply, sources for getting things made cheaply. And if you don't research the elements of design carefully, you can wind up spending hundreds or thousands of dollars extra in working on your space. For example, you can easily go to the finest fabric dealers and come away with treasures, but you can also achieve similar effects for far less money by researching outlet shops and discount houses where you can find fabrics equally attractive. You may not find the pattern you like in six different color screens, but so what? Won't four do? The difference in price will more than make up for the slight decrease in colors. *Extras*, finally, are those things you can't afford at the beginning that you allow yourself to project into the future. Everything from the Barcelona chair you have your heart set on instead of the thrift-shop bargain you wind up buying, to the fine accessories that are simply less vital initial purchases than, say, a set of coffee mugs or a bathroom scale. As to accessories, don't minimize their importance. There may be a world of difference between "design" and "decorating"—and designers may look down upon the merely decorative—but even the most excellent design can prove a flop if not properly accessorized. As we will see throughout this book, the strongest "statement" of your space will be its design; but the decorating of that space will be nonetheless important because it can either conflict with the basic design or enhance it.

Ultimately, you are the judge of what is right and correct about your space. Don't be so timid in your approach to design that you'll attempt to do only that which is pictured in books and magazines. You should not be afraid to make a statement, to exercise a little flair. After all, some of the most exciting elements of modern design are formally "incorrect." But so what? There are design projects in this book that are "incorrect." But of what value is someone else's opinion? In the end there is only one opinion that makes any difference, and that's your own. So do as you please, without worrying about what anyone else thinks, so long as your design satisfies you, so long as it's a genuine extension of yourself. For good design is intensely personal and even egotistical. Be yourself and don't be afraid. It may be perfectly elegant to be "correct," but it is just as "correct" to be strong in your statement. And by this I don't mean loud or glittery or sparkling or vulgar. I simply mean being honest in your feelings. In short, don't be oppressed by the merely fashionable. Don't be a marshmallow. Be yourself, hit upon what it is you want, and a design will emerge from your wants and desires so long as you are honest in projecting yourself.

*Illusion* and *camouflage* will prove important words in the pages that follow. If you're living in a dump, you don't necessarily feel that you *want* to be living in a dump. Hence, learning how to disguise artfully is a vital element of design. Effect is important. When you enter your apartment after walking through the dingy, dreadful hallways of your dump, you will want to feel like Dorothy having left Kansas for the wonderland of Oz. Your apartment, after all, is your very own personal stage. You are the director, the producer, the playwright—and especially the star. So hang everyone else, and don't be frightened of allowing your space to be an extension of your personality. Not every one of us is a Rembrandt, but all of us have played with Crayolas.

An excellent solution to the problem of storage space in a railroad flat: Turn an entire room into a combination dressing room/walk-in closet. Since the space leads directly from the room where guests enter to the combination living room/bedroom, the curved wall of corrugated metal divides the storage area from the "traffic path," so that guests do not feel as if they are walking through someone's closet.

# Storage

THINK OF STORAGE THIS WAY: You've just flown into a strange city and, shlepping an enormous suitcase, you've just checked into your hotel. Before you turn on the air-conditioner, before you even check to see whether the maid has left one of those cute, little paper bands around the toilet seat, you stash your bag where it is both accessible and out of the way. Now your hands are free, and you are free—free to do whatever it is you came to do in this strange city in the first place.

Dealing with storage space in your dump is just like that. In fact, storage should be your first object of consideration, because it is simply more important than any other element of design. In a sense, it is a clearing of the slate, for storage in a very real sense equals organization. The need for storage space simply forces you to be organized. And it doesn't make any difference whether you have one room or many. The question is still the same: Where are you going to stash the things you own? Your phonograph records are going to have to go somewhere. So will your towels and linens and clothing and groceries and books—and even your bicycle, if you happen to have one.

The trouble with most older dumps is that they're short on closets. Not only did people in the past own fewer possessions, but they stored them in large wardrobes and in trunks. So the likelihood is that you're going to walk head on into a major problem—a shortage, or a complete absence, of traditional storage space. Even before you lay out your space, you're going to have to cope with this all-encompassing problem. After you've dealt with it, you'll have cleared the slate and can move on to other things.

If you find yourself with a major storage problem, or if you simply need additional storage space, rethink everything that you're laying out in your apartment so that it can serve two or more functions. A coffee table, for example, can be more than a coffee table. If it has a drawer, it should be used to store

Don't despair when you stumble upon the wreck of a kitchen cabinet in your dump. As designer Leonard Braunschweiger has demonstrated, it can be turned into an elegant bookcase by applying new hardware, a can of paint, some basic carpentry skills, and more than a little bit of inventive fortitude.

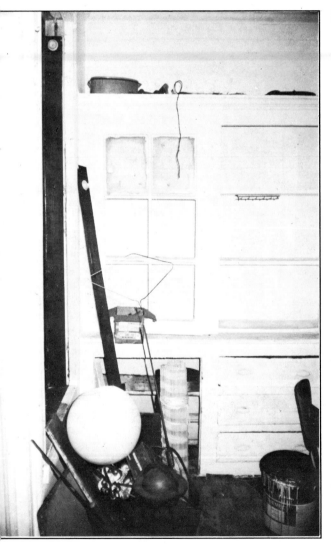

linens, say, or, if large enough, it can even house a bar. (Coffee tables with large drawers can be readily purchased in unpainted furniture stores.) If your space is small, you should force yourself to think about your need for storage before you buy even a single piece of furniture. And use decorative items, too, that would otherwise be merely decorative. Antique boxes and woven baskets, for example, make wonderful hiding places for commonly used objects.

The railroad flat of designer Leonard Braunschweiger (illustrated at the beginning of this chapter) incorporates the "ultimate" solution for storage because it uses a full room as a closet, a luxury that is suggested by the layout of the apartment itself (see the floor plan on page 84). You enter the flat through a room that functions as a combination workroom/dining room. The room that you enter next is a small space that leads directly to a combination living room/bedroom. The small room naturally suggests itself as a dressing room and functions both in that capacity and as a full-room closet. The ingeniously-designed curved wall is made of corrugated metal and divides the space used as a closet from the rest of the room. Since the room must serve as a passageway to the living room, the divider prevents guests from feeling that they are walking through a closet. The simple match-stick shade hides clothing and other stored items when guests are present.

   Illustrated on the opposite page (left) is the wreck of a cabinet that Leonard found when he moved into his tenement dump. It is typical of what you might find in yours—broken glass panes, missing doors and shelves, and ancient metal pulls that are covered with layer upon layer of old paint. The doors, of course, never open, and the drawers never close. Something to be tossed, you think. What Leonard did, however, is very clever. He removed the doors and added some inexpensive molding to the existing shelves to give them the appearance of having greater "substance," and he changed the hardware and replaced the missing drawers. The result (right) is a handsome bookcase rather than an ugly kitchen cabinet, a piece of furniture that is both elegant and inexpensive.

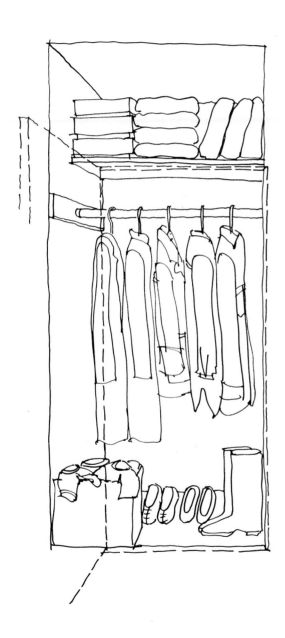

The typical clothes closet in most people's homes or apartments is a disaster area—a dump within a dump. Consisting of a single clothes pole and a single shelf, the closet (far left) is a jumble of piled objects on the shelf and a desert of wasted space above and below. A simple plan to turn your mess of a closet into a model of logic and order is illustrated at the left and is discussed within the text.

If you're lucky enough to have a closet in your dump, you'll probably find it fitted with a single clothes pole, with a shelf above and nothing below. In fact, if you open most people's closets, you'll discover a ton of stuff piled helter-skelter on the shelf, clothes hanging from the pole, and from eighteen inches to two feet of unused space between the pole and the shelf. The floor is usually a heap of shoes and whatever has fallen from the shelf above. A fantastic waste of space and a mess. Here's a suggestion about what can be done—and very simply and inexpensively.

Raise the clothes pole as high as you can. Install a shelf above it for dead storage space—for such rarely used items as suitcases and Christmas decorations. Since many closets are made much deeper than is necessary, take advantage of this space by moving the clothing rod farther back—at least nine inches from the back wall, which will give you eighteen inches for your hangers. Depending on where the door is located, you'll be left with additional space to the left or right, or, in some cases, on both sides. Use this space for the installation of narrow shelves, which will be perfect for storing T-shirts, socks, sweaters, and other articles of apparel. These shelves (especially if you live in a one-room dump) may save you the need of a chest of drawers. And they're better than drawers that force you to stack your things and which eventually become messy as you constantly pull things from the bottom. When you store your things on the narrow shelves of your newly organized closet, you can see them with no difficulty, and they will rarely become messy. This is a perfect example of "re-seeing" the events of your daily life. How many times do you open your present closet door and never even think about the wasted space? Rethink your life and do something about it. The closet is a good place to begin.

This simple plan of an organized closet is, in its own way, quite luxurious. By pushing the clothes pole far back in the closet, you create the not at all unpleasant sensation of having a walk-in closet. There's something about being able to lean into a closet when you go to retrieve something that makes it feel more spacious. It's a good feeling. Since most men's clothes are shirt length, there's room enough, actually, for two clothes poles. Coats (see illustration) can be hung from the top pole and stored in the space left between the pole and the wall. Finally, a simple shelf built for shoes will obviate the mess that is usually found on the closet floor.

With a little bit of ingenuity and an even smaller budget, you can turn a corner of a room into an elegant extended closet, as did designer Mel Hammock in his one-room studio apartment. By using inexpensive industrial shelving as a room divider to separate a preexisting closet from the rest of the room, and by backing it with birch plywood so that a new "wall" was formed in the main part of the room, he created the wonderful dressing room pictured above (right). The original closet is incorporated into the design of the dressing room, since clothing is hung on the left side while the center portion is reserved for a dresser. The inexpensive clip-on lighting fixtures are arranged uniformly face down for a dramatic effect.

*Opposite page:* Inexpensive store-bought shelving, used with imagination and with flair, can create delightful storage areas that belie their own low cost. Standard wall shelving (left), if unstained and placed against a dark background, is particularly dramatic. The brackets, painted the dark color of the walls, become "invisible" and allow the shelves to "float." The dressing room at the right is carved from the corner of a studio apartment by using a room divider of industrial shelves.

*Left:* Since very few bathrooms in dumps have sufficient storage space, it's relatively easy to construct shelving that provides not only a place to hide such common articles as soap and scouring powder, but allows ample counter space as well. The simple store-bought curtain does away with the need for expensive cabinetry.

In the main part of his studio (opposite, left), a similar idea for storage is incorporated. Typical store-bought shelves on metal brackets support handsome woven bags that serve as attractive places for storing objects. The simple pine shelves are left a light pine color and are not stained walnut, as is so frequently the case. (Pine has a beauty of its own, so why pretend it's something that it's not?) In this ground-floor apartment, made gloomy by security bars across its windows, the walls are painted black to "go with" the handicap of being naturally dark. By taking advantage of the apartment's shortcomings, the designer has created a particularly dramatic effect that is both intense and exciting.

The entrance to photographer Peter M. Fine's loft in an industrial building is directly off the street. As a transition from the warehouse-like atmosphere of the building to his finished loft, he decided to create an entrance foyer that retained the industrial look of his neighborhood. The foyer is set up to simulate a warehouse and consists of props—a mop and pail as "sculpture," a receiving desk, and a wall of packing crates on industrial skids. As the illustration at the left shows, these packing crates actually serve as a witty and ingenious storage area. Within the boxes are frames that hold shelves for objects used around the apartment—from *real* mops and cleaning paraphernalia to paint cans and even a bicycle. Even the stencils on the boxes are artfully done. The entire effect is very clever, very inexpensive.

The simple bathroom pictured on the previous page is in a country house, but it illustrates a good way in which to treat a bathroom anywhere. Here the walls are covered with barn wood found on the property, but crate wood could be used just as simply. (Although crate wood lacks a handsome patina, it does possess an interesting texture which shows through the paint that must of necessity cover it.) Like most bathrooms in dumps, the sink was completely without any storage or counter space. But it was located in an alcove which made building a shelf around it an easy task. Below the sink is a curtain that hides additional shelves for storage. Not only is there sufficient room for towels and toilet items, but the shelves do away with the need for an expensive medicine cabinet. The unpainted barn-wood shelf above the sink to the left allows the display of show towels.

Just the few examples pictured on these pages should be sufficient to demonstrate the almost endless ways in which the need for space, combined with human ingenuity, can create unique storage areas. Of these many solutions to an age-old problem, surely the packing-crate closets pictured on the opposite page must be some sort of *ne plus ultra!*

The furnishings of this one-room brownstone apartment are either made by hand or acquired by "trading up," a process that requires patience and a willingness to bring together a design over an extended period of time. By beginning with basic pieces of furniture, and selling these once additional money is available, and by diligently scouting thrift shops and flea markets, you, too, can trade up and create a strong statement that is uniquely your own.

# Furniture

Now that you've cleaned your slate and have given considerable thought to where you are going to store the articles that you use during the course of your typical day, it's time to turn your attention to furniture. Why furniture at this juncture and not, say, layout when you haven't yet decided formally where things are going to go in your space? Because most people bring to a new space furniture that they already own—furniture that is brought along because you love it or because you simply can't afford *not* to bring it with you. Since you have to be aware of these pieces before you design your layout, this is also the time to plan those additional pieces that you *must* have. After all, you *have* to eat, so you're going to need a table to dine at. And you have to sleep and have to sit, and perhaps you even have to work within the confines of your walls. So that means beds and chairs and even desks. Obviously, there are certain "givens" that have to be dealt with before one can progress to layouts.

Furniture, bought in the traditional manner, means money, lots of money. And built-in pieces, by now a bit of a design cliché anyway, is not particularly practical for denizens of dumps since the landlord is likely to tell you at any moment that the wreckers' ball is on its way to blast your little spot of clay into a 47-story high-rise. So let's look at the alternatives: furniture that you scout out at flea markets and junk shops, furniture that you build yourself from scratch or from found objects, and furniture that you buy from discount stores and other outlets.

My own one-room dump, pictured on the opposite page, is a perfect case in point. It demonstrates what can come from haunting flea markets, "trading up," and building one's own pieces. Even though the apartment's contents seem to be "standard"—a sofa, an ottoman, a coffee table, a chair, a number of assorted pillows—they are not the sort of apartment furnishings that you can find in a department store. Nor can you simply run out to the nearest flea market and duplicate the pieces. What you have to do is

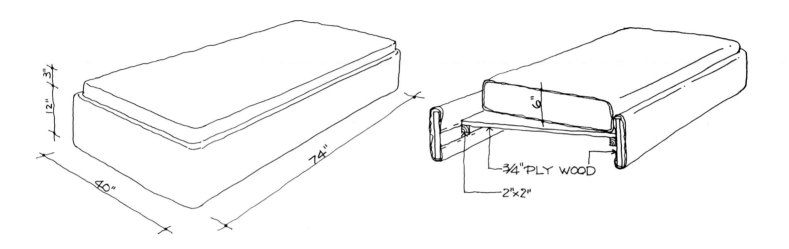

By following the scheme of this drawing, you can reproduce the sofa illustrated on page 72. And it's easy to make, since it is only a frame into which the mattress of a single bed is made to fit. Measure your mattress and allow about an extra inch for the dimensions of the frame. Resting on plywood supported by two-by-twos, the mattress should sit about two inches below the sides of the plywood. The frame itself is composed of five pieces of 3/4"-plywood, nailed and glued together. As drawn here, the sofa is intentionally basic, but there is no reason why arms or a back cannot be added. But be honest in your adaptation. This is not intended to be a luxurious sofa, so don't try to make it look like one. Its charm stems from the fact that it is merely a mattress on a platform.

to be willing to start out with certain basic furnishings—and then trade up. Being patient and slowly trading up are absolute keys to furnishing your dump inexpensively. When you start out, whatever else you do, don't yield to the impulse of buying everything *new*. And, for goodness' sake, don't be an idiot and invest in a store-bought suite of machine-made furniture. Be patient and live with a few basic essentials until you can do better by selling those pieces and trading up. If you don't have the "right sofa," or can't afford the sofa that you really want, don't make the mistake of doing without a sofa at all. Buy something that you can live with, something basic, and wait until you can sell what you have, add a little money to your proceeds, and then buy something better. Make certain that you buy pieces that you can later sell for at least the money that you paid for them. And run apartment or garage sales when the right time comes along.

My coffee table cost me less than five dollars. Originally a dining room table that someone had cut down to a very odd height, it makes a convenient coffee table now that its legs have been shortened even more. The sofa—essentially a standard mattress sunk within a frame—is homemade and simple enough for anyone to build (see the drawings on the opposite page). Everyone should have one of these! Essentially a single bed, it seats four when used as a sofa and sleeps one. The black chair is one of two originally from a barber shop that cost me fifty dollars for the pair. The fabric covering the sofa (a satin faille) would probably retail for an even hundred a yard if purchased new, but I bought twenty-five yards of it at a flea market for eight dollars. It had been someone's draperies. Naturally, you're not going to come up with bargains such as these every time you go out hunting, but it pays to visit thrift shops and other bargain basements constantly. Keep looking and you'll eventually find the pieces that you want.

As home-built projects go, the sofa is a relative breeze. Made from only a mattress and five pieces of plywood, plus a pair of two-by-twos, it does not require professional upholstering. Just staple upholstery batting to the frame, and then staple on a fabric of your choice. As to upholstering the mattress itself, simply take a flat piece of fabric and tuck it in! So what if it gets mussed up when you sit on it. So do good down pillows. In fact, it's good for things to get mussed up, to get crushed. It's a quality that gives an apartment life. (Is there anything worse than a hard foam pillow that is immobile and dead?) Messy

A new lease on life has been given to these discarded objects—two metal-tubed kitchen chairs and the frame of a lawn or beach chair—by placing them within fitted sacks. The sacks are made of cotton duck, which is both inexpensive and strong. What's more, duck won't stretch, a factor particularly important for the beach chair which requires support. Use of the wrong fabric could cause your butt to sag like the rickety pier in this witty photograph.

things can actually be luxurious. Just tuck in the upholstery fabric again after your guests leave, and relax. Like furnishings discovered through diligent searches of flea markets and thrift shops, the piece of furniture joined at home with nails and glue and ingenuity can provide far more enjoyment anf flair than the matched set bought on credit at a tony high-priced department store.

The idea of "going junking" may not particularly appeal to you in theory, but in actuality it's amazing what potential furnishings you can find discarded on the streets. Whole apartments have been furnished with the detritus of our throw-away society, and the following pages will demonstrate a few examples of what can be done with the imagination that is born of a desire to save money. What can be done, to say the least, is extraordinary.

A case in point are the chairs illustrated on the opposite page. The "givens" here are two different types of discarded furniture, one a Breuer-like kitchen chair typical of the 1930s and '40s, the other the frame of a beach or deck chair. Designer Bruce Bierman took these unloved objects, made sacks that fit over them, and turned them into fascinating and useful pieces of furniture. In so doing, he has imbued them with a completely different quality. They seem almost like people; one imagines that they are capable of walking off on their own. This remarkable transformation is an excellent example of what I mean by "re-seeing." The designer has seen pieces of discarded junk and immediately envisioned them as serviceable furniture.

Just how all-encompassing this notion of "re-seeing" can be is easily demonstrated by the nine examples of furniture made from "found objects" that appear on the following pages. The objects created were the result of a three-week interior design assignment at New York's Fashion Institute of Technology, under the supervision of Professor Julius Panero. Students were requested to explore junkyards, construction sites, refuse containers, and other seemingly unpromising places for objects that, for whatever reason, seemed particularly interesting to them. They were then to adapt the objects selected so that they would function as elements of interior furniture or as lighting. The project was conceived as an exercise in creativity, problem solving, form, and structure, but it may be viewed as well as an exercise in re-seeing. If a poet may be defined as a person who sees relationships in things that other people fail to see, then these nine objects are most certainly the work of incipient poets of design.

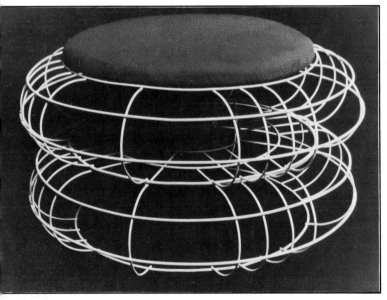

*Above, left:* Child's chair with tilting table, designed by Carmen Rodriguez, and constructed from a discarded gas tank from a truck. *Above, right:* Chair, designed by Michael Mafrici, and constructed from the exposed refrigeration coils of a discarded refrigerator. *Left:* Hassock/cocktail table combination, designed by Ann Strait, and constructed from the wire safety enclosure of an electric fan. The padded plywood seat is removable and can be replaced by a piece of plexiglas when it is to serve as a table.

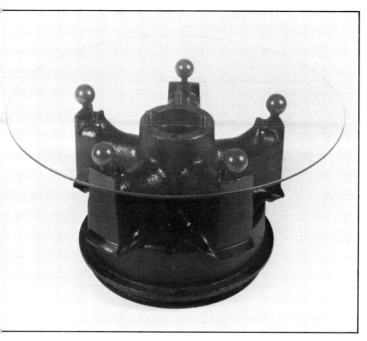

*Above, left:* Cocktail table, designed by Peter Shu, and constructed from a discarded 24″-diameter truck rim. Red paddle balls fastened to protruding lug bolts of the rim support a circular ¼″ glass table top. Red tape secured to the edge of the glass acts to underscore the form of the table. *Above, right:* Combination magazine rack and table, designed by Gail Huber, and constructed by adapting two discarded merchandise display stands. The upper stand was placed bottom-side up and secured to the lower stand with a plexiglas shaft. The shaft is filled with black gravel to stabilize the table. The assembly is painted white. The top of the table is ½″ plexiglas. *Left:* Cocktail table, designed by Robert Vecchione, and constructed from a discarded winch. The cable was removed and the winch placed on its side. Its various elements were painted in bright, playful colors. A circular piece of ½″ plexiglas serves as the table top.

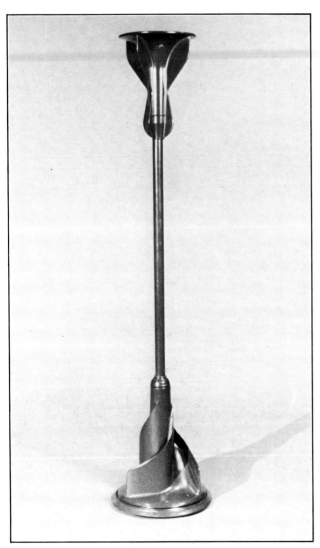

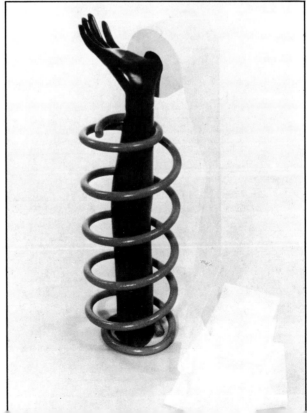

*Far left*: Floor lamp, designed by Susan Trenkner. Two discarded washing machine agitators, linked by a length of PVG pipe, were painted and fashioned into an elegant floor lamp. *Above, left*: Multifunctional hassock/pedestal, designed by Zvia Drogoshinsky, and constructed from discarded automobile wheel rims stacked one above the other. Two-rims high, and with a padded piece of circular plywood, the rims function as a seat. Three-rims high or more, the rims function as a pedestal for plants or other objects. *Below, left*: Tissue paper dispenser, designed by Joan Zennock. A discarded shock absorber coil and mannequin arm were fashioned into a paper dispenser to add an element of humor to the decor of a bathroom.

The dining area of a modern apartment designed by David Hecht uses furniture from the budget line of a major manufacturer. By scouting the scores of outlet shops and discount centers that have sprung up along the highways of America's largest population areas, you can take advantage of the bargain of the moment, but arranging the objects with the artistic subtlety of Mr. Hecht is another matter altogether. For another view of how he has considerably warmed up an essentially cold apartment, see page 52.

Finally, there is store-bought furniture. Just as professional designers working on a tight budget avail themselves of "budget" furniture made by the leading manufacturers and available only to the trade, you can take advantage of the budget lines carried by many department stores and other outlets. And then, of course, there are discontinued lines, floor samples, and what appears to be miles and miles of unpainted furniture available from coast to coast. What is involved here is diligence and research and patience. In short, the eyes of an eagle and that fabled bird's ability to swoop down like lightning at the moment you discern a bargain.

Another view of the apartment designed by David Hecht. Using furniture from a manufacturer's discount line, the designer breaks step with the usual layout in a modern, lifeless apartment by floating one sofa out into the room and creating a delightful sitting area. Just because the modern living room gives you only one unbroken wall for your sofa is no reason to place it there automatically or to use only one. If you allow yourself to be intimidated by the ordinary, then you are at least as boring as the architect who designed the boring building that you're living in.

# Layout

PROBABLY THE MOST essential aspect of design, but certainly the most frequently ignored by otherwise intelligent people, is the floor plan, that architectural shorthand that defines the layout of a space just as surely as musical notation defines the structure of a symphony. If the vision of carrying random pieces of furniture up five flights of stairs and then carting them around your dump to determine where they might best "go" does not appeal to you, then you'd better buckle down to the importance, and convenience of a floor plan. Putting one together will keep you glued to your desk for an hour or two, but the effort will be more than worth your while.

Everyone should have an "empty" floor plan of his apartment. Start with a sheet of graph paper. Drawing to scale, with a ruler, is really far more simple than you think. Each one of the little squares should represent a foot or six inches or whatever scale you choose. Start by measuring the farthest distance between points in your room. This will help you to determine the scale of your drawing, since you do not want your drawing to suddenly "fall off" the graph paper because it couldn't accommodate the longest or widest dimension of your flat. Make certain to indicate where all doors and windows appear, or any place where it would prove impossible to place a piece of furniture or to build a shelf. Map this all out in pencil or in ink, and then you have an empty floor plan. Do this room by room and join all the rooms together.

Once you have your floor plan prepared, the next step, even if you have only one room, is to block out areas by function. This means, of course, reviewing your questions about your lifestyle. You have to eat, you have to sleep, you have to work, etc. And think out where the most logical places will be to exercise these functions. Start with big blocks of space to define functions before you even attempt to map out where your furniture will go. Function, after all, will determine just what furniture is needed where.

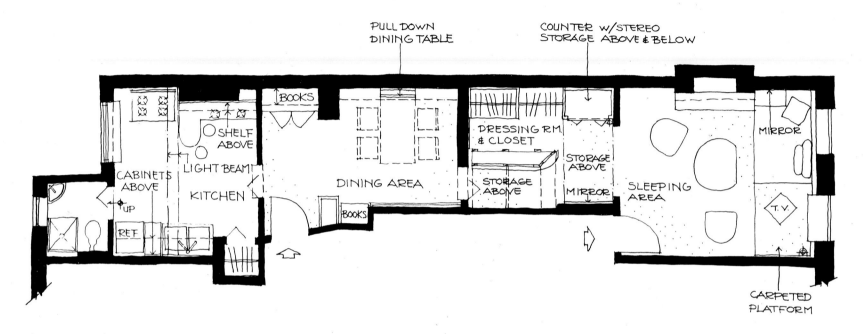

The layout of designer Leonard Braunschweiger's railroad apartment is perfection of its kind. Even though the kitchen and bathroom are obviously fixed—as they are in most apartments—virtually every space in the flat has multiple functions. The room that one enters on coming through the front door serves as a dining room or workroom, and, as the photographs on the following pages show, the room can even remain completely open for whatever purpose one wishes it to have. The dressing room that this runs into has already been discussed and is pictured on page 62. This runs, in turn, into the multifunctional living room/sleeping area. The apartment is laid out with economy and logic. It can be readily used for comfortable living, entertaining, and for work when that proves necessary.

Take a piece of tracing paper and work with pencil over your drawing if you don't want to have to continually erase. Then start blocking out the different areas on the tracing paper until you hit upon an arrangement that makes the most logical sense to you. Before you know it, a floor plan will begin to emerge. Map out traffic paths. Map out doorways and other places where furnishings would cause obstructions. In examining your plan, figure out how to create privacy, an important element in any design. Will dividers be necessary?

Obviously, you will have to ask yourself all sorts of personal questions as you map out your plan. And you'll need a good eraser on your pencil. Details will change constantly until you're satisfied. As you start to block out where furniture is to go, you will almost "see" what is going to happen to the pieces. Will you have to walk around something because it's been placed in the path of traffic? Is a piece of furniture too large for the space where you originally intended it? All this will become clear to you if you map things out before you actually move them. It even helps sometimes to build scale models of your furniture out of paper, moving them around the floor plan to get a better idea of how things will look in certain places. But first, of course, you start with big blocks of space according to function. You don't start by asking yourself where you're going to put the sofa. That's not particularly important. You start by asking yourself where your guests are going to sit. Where you're going to pay your monthly bills. Where you're going to sleep. The better you know yourself, the better your floor plan will be. But even after you move into your dump, as you force yourself to be more and more aware of your needs and habits, you will eventually move things around in your space so that the layout continually improves to the point where everything begins to function perfectly.

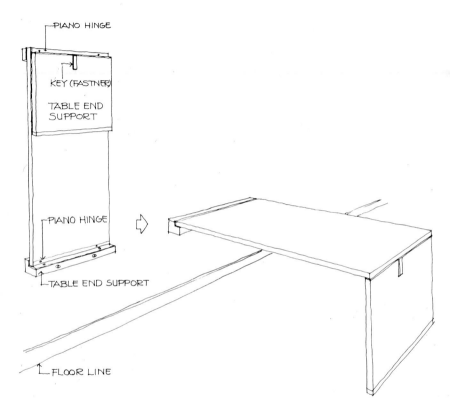

PIANO HINGE

KEY (FASTNER)

TABLE END
SUPPORT

PIANO HINGE

TABLE END SUPPORT

FLOOR LINE

Leonard Braunschweiger's multipurpose dining room/ workroom/reception room features a handsome retractable table that makes it possible for the room to function in any capacity. It consists of two planes that come down on two piano hinges that open up. When open, the smaller plane becomes the second leg of the table, the support on the wall acting as the first. When closed, it functions as a beautifully painted sculpture. This simple idea for a table may be adapted to whatever use you wish—from a writing desk to a dining table.

In this studio apart-
ment, a badly cracked
ceiling is artfully
camouflaged by
marbleizing—applying
layers of different col-
ored paints with
sponges and stippling
brushes. The eye is
thereby deflected from
the cracked ceiling. The
spot of light on the
flowers in a vase further
distracts the eye. The
total effect of the
background statement
is high drama.

# Backgrounds

By NOW, with a little bit of luck and with a great deal of serious introspection and forthright questioning, you should have a completed floor plan—"complete" in that it can begin to take shape in the future, even though you might not yet have all the pieces of furniture that you plan on eventually having. Now the work begins. Starting with a few pieces of well-selected furniture, and with a good, strong, solid background, you can now create the ambience of your design in progress. By "background," I mean ceilings, walls, and floors. And it's backgrounds that can make the strongest statement in a room while containing the fewest elements.

Take the color illustration on the opposite page, for example. This is the work of interior designer Thom Deligter. He employs a very strong background and only a few carefully selected pieces of furniture, but the effect is immediately dramatic. When he moved into his large studio apartment, the ceiling was badly cracked and peeling. What he did, essentially, was to scrape off all the loose paint, but he attempted very little plastering. His plan called for him to add layer after layer of different colored paints to create a marble-like or cloudlike effect. Consequently, the ceiling of his room has become its focal point, and no one would ever guess the wretched condition that it was in originally. A beautiful statement, it cost him only about $100 to bring off. Had he followed a more orthodox route—sanding, plastering, etc.—it would have cost him anywhere from five to six times that amount to achieve an effect far more conventional and far less individualistic than this. Ironically, the designer was working on a limited budget, a point which hammers home the truth of the old observation that necessity is the mother of invention. Working together with a friend, the designer applied the various paints to the ceiling with sponges and with stippling brushes. If you want to pursue this effect, you might want to check out any one of several how-to books on the market that discuss the technique of marbleizing (or marbling). Or you might simply try it out on your own by experimenting on a small area of ceiling. It's not that difficult to figure out how it's done on your own. Incidentally, notice how Thom Deligter has painted the moldings white, a touch that emphasizes not only the architectural details of the room, but also the unusual ceiling itself.

In dumps, floors are generally made of hardwood that has long seen better days. Usually in deplorable condition, they have been painted over time and time again or covered over with layers of linoleum that, more often than not, have adhered viscously to the surface. Another common problem is that precious few floors are straight. If you lay a roller skate at one end of a room, it is very likely to roll its way to the other end as soon as you turn your back. What to do for the latter problem? If the angle is dramatically acute, or if the lumps and bumps are really getting to you, you can always lay another floor over it. Or you can build a platform, which would prove particularly advantageous where things must be on the level—as in a dining area. Another thing to do, especially if the problem is not severe, is to prop up the wobbly leg or legs of your furniture with lucite blocks. Available in many stores that specialize in selling plastic products, such blocks enable the furniture to be level without the block being seen. Wooden blocks under furniture legs not only disfigure the lines of a piece, but they give it the appearance of having a clubfoot.

Floors are frequently the most expensive investment in an apartment. But, like shoes in a complete outfit of clothing, they frequently ruin the total design. All too many people, even residents of dumps, rely on cheap carpeting to end their flooring woes. But cheap is cheap, and such carpeting always looks cheap, not "inexpensive." Don't waste your money. Rather than invest in good carpeting, which is boring and ordinary at best and almost always looks preposterous in old settings, why not simply paint your floor? The texture of the wood will still come through, and may very well appear far less pretentious than a floor stripped down to its so-called "natural" wood. (In many cases, if you *do* attempt stripping, you may discover after a great deal of backbreaking work that the wood was hardly "quality" to begin with and was originally meant to be covered.) In any event, a painted floor is far more interesting in a really dumpy dump than a modern carpeted or tiled floor, for it adds warmth to a room without being as heavy or as ponderous as carpeting or as medicinal as vinyl tile. You can always add area rugs, or mats, or large pillows for the comfort of friends who enjoy sitting on the floor at a gathering or a party. If you don't want to paint your floor a single color, you can paint alternate rows of squares or diamonds in a checkerboard pattern of two different colors. This effect can simulate tile or simply create an interesting optical effect, as was common in many 18th- and 19-century American rooms. You can also stencil a floor to paint a fake "carpet" on it. Or you can cover part of your floor with a cheap sisal rug and paint an elaborate fringe on it. This whimsical touch can add a touch of class to an otherwise cheap object by satirizing the luxuriousness of an expensive rug, a high-priced item that you might covet but can't really afford. Needless to say, there are hundreds of other design stratagems that can be devised.

Because walls and ceilings are generally more visible than floors, they are without doubt the biggest problem of living in a dump. In old buildings they are usually peeling and cracked. And there's not much that you can do about this problem since, in many cases, they are going to continue to peel and crack no matter what you do to them. Perhaps the "farthest out" thing that you can do to them is to merely let them peel. One person I know actually did this. He totally lacquered the walls with a very shiny paint, while the ceiling continued to peel, taking on a texture all its own. Obviously, this "solution" is not for everyone. But it's one way to do it.

When impeded by such obstacles as terrible walls and ceilings, you either lick them or join them. That is, you either go with them or against them. If you choose to go totally against them, you could, say, cover the ceiling with fabric and drape the walls as well. Draping fabric (see the illustration on page 23) is far easier to do than you would think. You can nail a wooden molding around the room and staple the fabric to it, or you can hang it from rods, a method that would enable you to take the fabric off for cleaning.

Whatever else you do, avoid commercial dropped ceilings at all cost. Not only is material expensive, but why on earth would you want your place to resemble an insurance office or a finished basement in a suburban tract? If you must drop the ceiling, at least do it inventively, as in the room illustrated on page 110. Or you could cover the ceiling with Homosote—a heavy cardboard-like substance—to which fabric has been attached. Covered in squares of fabric-covered Homosite, the ceiling takes on a uniquely upholstered look. This can be effective on walls, as well.

One overdone solution to cracked walls is the use of plaster stucco. What you're really doing if you stucco your walls is hiding the lumps and bumps by adding *more* lumps and bumps. Cork panels are also a cliché. Why not try wood crating instead? Rather than living with a pizza-parlor look, you can have something infinitely more inventive. I once covered walls with corrugated cardboard and painted it. Once covered with an oil-base paint, the rippled cardboard resists crushing and creates a wonderful texture by appearing very much like expensive striae.

Objects covering an entire wall can work, too. One person took antique picture frames and created interesting patterns on the walls with them. The object, obviously, is to cover the poor texture of the original wall with a more interesting texture. Plain brown wrapping paper is wonderful, too. Hung as wallpaper, it has an exciting texture of its own to recommend it. And it's cheap. If your walls are especially bumpy, brown paper hung in overlapping strips can effectively camouflage the walls and look terrific on its own. You can also use aluminum foil in a similar way. Overlap it in strips, using rubber cement to make it adhere as wallpaper. Then cover it with a coat of polyurethane. It will appear almost like silver leaf. Dazzling, yes, but remember that Andy Warhol practically patented this idea a million years ago. So why not limit your use of aluminum foil to trim alone? Remember, too, that there are wallpapers sold commercially that are made specifically to cover bad walls. And then, of course, there's paint. Good old paint. In the right color, or combination of colors, paint can create the depth of velvet. If your walls are salvageable—if thay *can* be repaired—then there's nothing to equal a good paint job. (See the illustration on page 122, for example.) Even if your walls remain cracked, you can "exploit" the cracks by learning how to marbleize the walls with paint. This will effectively camouflage them and create a dramatic statement.

*Camouflage.* That magic word again. If you're living in a dump, why not distract the eye from the walls, rather than attracting it to them? Paint the walls a dark color and they will actually recede. If you then pin-spot a painting, or a piece of sculpture, or a flower in a vase, you can distract the eye still further. But this is leading us to the uses of lighting, a subject that will soon be discussed.

Working on a limited budget, designers Nicholas Politis and Richard Des Jardins transformed a dark and dingy beach house into a minor miracle of color. Finding the existing paneling darkened with the years to an excruciating orange, they mixed turpentine and sea-foam green paint and rubbed it into the wood, a process they call "pickling." The result is a background of subtle beauty. By adding pillows, comforters, and sheets—all colorful—the rooms come alive. Here color suggests richness, even though the costs were minimal. Even the choice of a parson's table covered in formica makes all the difference because of its uncommon color. White would have been dull, ordinary. Because the color is unusual and rich, it suggests that the table is far more expensive than it really is.

# Color

LET'S BE HONEST. Entire tomes have been written, and will continue to be written, about the psychology of color. It is an enormous subject, and one fraught with peril, because color is observed differently by everyone. Yet, despite its relativity, color is a subject that seems to invite the greatest number of ironclad rules and regulations about what is and is not permissible in the world of rainbow hues. Even though these rules seem to bend with the comings and goings of current fashion, every generation allows itself to be tyrannized by the existence of that *arbiter elegantiarum*, the Color Wheel—and its do's and don'ts, its yeas and nays, its maybe's and sort-of's, and occasional perhapses. If you'd like to consult a color wheel, almost every book on the basics of design reproduces one; but prepare yourself for an accompanying list of moral strictures considerably longer than the Ten Commandments.

So far as I'm concerned—and purists may want to hang me from the highest yardarm—there are only two rules to be followed regarding color:

*First rule:* There is no such thing as an ugly color.
*Second rule:* What can be ugly are certain combinations of colors.

Since there is no such thing as an ugly color, try to move away from the traditional combinations of colors that have become design clichés: such combinations as blue and green, for example, or beige and orange. Because current fashion has so drilled us in these colors, they have limited us in our choices.

When it comes to selecting colors for your dump, the essence of my experience can be distilled as follows:

The different colors that you put together,
The amounts of those different colors,

And the light in which those colors are going to be seen
—these are the important things to consider.

Everything else useful (and not just theoretical) that I can pass on to you about color relates to this basic observation.

It's amazing what colors can do to one another. You can fall in love with a color, but the moment you bring it into your own home the other objects that you have will make it appear to be totally different from what you originally saw. When you examine a color in a paint store, don't examine it in artificial light (for some strange reason usually fluorescent). Take the chip outside or at least look at it by the window or the door. And even this will not be foolproof. After all, your apartment is not exactly outdoors. The fact is, you won't know what that color will look like until you see it at home. Actually, don't ever paint until you buy a small sample of the paint and try it on the wall. It can look totally different in the light of your space than you thought it would.

Another thing, if you're trying to see how colors are going to look together—say, a fabric and a paint selected for the walls—then see the color and the fabric in proportional relation to one other. If a single chair is going to be covered with the fabric, but the whole room is going to be painted with the paint, then don't make a judgment by examining a tiny paint chip and an enormous swatch of fabric. The proportions should be exactly the other way around. Just because the colors go nicely together when seen together in the same size doesn't mean that they're going to look as well when the diminutive chair is seen against a huge wall of color.

If one were to judge what is current fashion by examining the model rooms pictured in department store catalogues, then one would imagine that it was *infra dig* to decorate your space in anything but matching fabrics—the same pattern on the walls, chairs, draperies, beds, and on and on and on. In looking at these rooms that resemble mummies swathed in designer bandages, one wants to scream, "Why, oh why, oh why?" When you have six pieces of furniture in a room and fifteen different surfaces, why on earth would you want everything to match? When rooms, even in a dump, look so "planned," it's an absolute turn-off. Things in a well-designed room should appear as if they are somehow happening, not as if they've been planned to happen. Each time I see one of those matching ensembles so beloved of department stores and magazine editors, I want to hand the designers a friendly can of paint, in a contrasting color, and say, "Loosen up a little, damn it."

Related to the subject of color is the touchy matter of mixing different patterned prints. This is one of the most difficult (and certainly the most scary) elements of design, because there are really no rules at all to follow. There are some basic clues, however. Usually it's safe to couple many of the same things together—like stripes, or florals, or plaids. And if they're approximately the same size, or of similar coloring, that's all to the better. The problems begin when patterns of drastically different sizes are mixed together, even though they're of the same type—a large plaid with a small plaid, for example, or a large floral with a small floral. Apparently, it's O.K. to mix patterned prints of the same type if the differences in size are only somewhat different, but it becomes "weird" when the differences in size are extreme.

Since you've already considered your layout and your furniture, the "mood" of your room is already set, thereby limiting your choice of colors. Therefore, when it comes time to select the items in your room that will eventually determine its color scheme, start with whatever item is most limited in the marketplace. Since there are obviously fewer rugs in this world than fabrics, purchase your area rug *before* you select your fabrics. Similarly, select your fabrics before you choose your paint. In this way, your choice of rug will help to predetermine your choice of paint. But don't be too literal about this. Don't try to match the *exact* colors of the rug with the colors of your paints. This would be too artificial, too lifeless. Colors that are slightly "off" are infinitely more human than exact matches. Just make certain that the rug doesn't wind up looking totally out of place because you forgot about it in selecting your other colors.

From this point, you're on your own. To summarize: Don't have any fear in using color. If *you* think it looks good, then it looks good.

This window treatment illustrates the mixing of different prints for effect. Although the combination of prints, patterns, and textures is unconventional, it works in creating a strong statement of individuality. All the fabrics were found in thrift shops, including one fine pillow that is covered in silk. The result of blending one expensive object with several inexpensive pieces is startling: the good seems to raise the stock of the ordinary. The lushness of the fabrics is in sharp relief to the simply painted architectural trim of the window itself, while the flower placed *outside* the window creates an outdoor environment to be seen from within, a particularly effective device if the view from your dump is depressingly dull.

# Windows

RUMPY. That's what most window treatments are. You know the look. It has hardly changed in thirty years of January white sales: a gauzy undercurtain, usually in white and just as usually of an easily washable synthetic like fiberglas; and a set of store-bought draperies on a drawstring traverse rod, frequently a shiny acrylic "antique satin" or an open-weave synthetic or a flowered or a patterned print. When open, such ready-made draperies don't look too bad, although they do tend to frame the window like two rigid sentinels on guard. When drawn, however, they're an incongruous mass of cloth across the wall, a claustrophobic blindfold that closes off the rest of the world and diminishes the room. Either way, they're almost always too short or too long and almost never just right, unless you're particularly talented at sewing hems.

If you live in an old dump, the windows are frequently the most handsome architectural feature. The frames, though buried under layers of old paint, are often beautifully molded, and even the simplest sometimes boast bulls-eye corner blocks. More often than not, windows in dumps are taller than those in new buildings and provide a hint of luxury and fine workmanship absent in most contemporary settings. Why, then, would anyone want to hide these architectural assets under yards of regulation fabric? Any way you look at it, few things look tackier in an aging dump than the standard department-store window treatment. If the many spaces pictured in this book share one thing in common, it's the absence of drawstring draperies. There are simple sheer curtains (if there are window coverings at all), Venetian blinds, tab curtains, and even old-fashioned window shades, but there are no store-bought draperies on traverse rods. And this is hardly an accident. They simply look preposterously suburban in a city dump—or in any period setting for that matter.

*Left*: A pleasant window treatment can be achieved by draping a single piece of fabric about a standard window pole. This softens the architecture of the window without sacrificing too much of the light that is admitted. There is no one particular way to drape the fabric, and you can attain whatever effect you wish if you use a piece of fabric that is sufficiently long. You can also change your window treatment as the spirit moves you, an option that can't be had with standard draperies that are more or less fixed in place. *Right*: A sense of privacy can be attained by the use of a window box placed *inside* the window. Plans for window boxes built outside tenement windows are illustrated on pages 44 and 47.

Unless you're the sort who is happiest parading around the house *au naturel*, there's really no need to waste your money on elaborate window treatments. You can actually do very well without curtains of any kind, leaving the window frames completely undraped. A plant or two can provide a sense of privacy and tone down the harshness of the bare architectural details. If you're occasionally bothered by nosy neighbors or if you're up to something pleasantly indecent, you can always turn out the lights. Better still, and especially if your apartment benefits from plenty of sunshine, why not install window shades? They're not only inexpensive, but perfectly in keeping with the period "feel" of most dumps.

There are, needless to say, entire books on window treatments, and, if you want to go whole hog, you should consult them. But my point, of course, is that you needn't break the bank to create unusual window treatments, inexpensive designs that provide privacy or the impression of privacy and a point of interest. Additional ideas regarding "window landscaping" may be found on pages 44 and 47. All of these suggestions, naturally, are copyright-free and viable alternatives to the department-store-catalogue look that you should go out of your way to eschew.

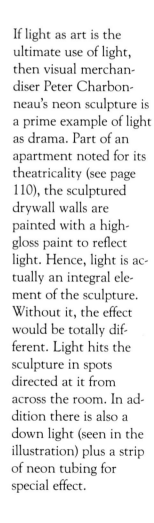

If light as art is the ultimate use of light, then visual merchandiser Peter Charbonneau's neon sculpture is a prime example of light as drama. Part of an apartment noted for its theatricality (see page 110), the sculptured drywall walls are painted with a high-gloss paint to reflect light. Hence, light is actually an integral element of the sculpture. Without it, the effect would be totally different. Light hits the sculpture in spots directed at it from across the room. In addition there is also a down light (seen in the illustration) plus a strip of neon tubing for special effect.

# Lighting

OVERSIMPLIFIED as this might at first seem, lighting can be broken down into three basic purposes. The first, the most obvious, and the most misused is simply to illuminate—to provide light. The second is to direct the eye—to force it to focus on something. And the third is to create a particular atmosphere or mood—to create drama. Most of us rarely get beyond the first function, and most almost never progress to the second and the third because of what I call the "snow blindness syndrome." Most people keep their spaces so flooded with intense light that, if artificial light were the sun itself, we'd all of us be charred to a crisp. Such brilliant light, bad enough in an office or a fast-food emporium, is sheer torture in a residence. And it's not only unnecessary and aesthetically unpleasant to some, but costly to all. Have you looked at your electricity bill lately? Have you ever heard of a utility rate that went *down*?

If your dump is lit like an operating room, if even the roaches seem to be wearing sunglasses, then why not consider that clever little gismo called the dimmer? Far from being merely a toy for decorators or a tony gadget for "fancy people," a dimmer can solve your problems with lighting's Category One and provide your entrée to Category Three. By installing dimmers on the switches to all your ceiling fixtures and table lamps, you can move from dazzling illumination to soft and dramatic lighting that changes with your moods and with the functions of your space. And the money that you save on your electricity bill will eventually pay for the dimmers themselves. Here is the perfect lighting compromise. Just a turn of the dimmer and you are ready to enjoy casual conversation, a "candle-lit" dinner, dramatic entertaining, or enough illumination to read a book comfortably. And, if you're completely unregenerate in your love of intense light, the dimmer will still allow you enough wattage to perform brain surgery on the kitchen table, if you're so inclined.

Two examples of inexpensive lighting fixtures made by folding plain brown wrapping paper. The first—a wall fixture that is pierced—creates an umbra of yellow light against the brown paper, a beautiful effect. The second is a hanging fixture that directs light below.

As to the second aspect of light – light that directs the eye – have you ever watched how sunlight at a certain time of day hits objects in a room, or is refracted through a prism, or a beveled mirror, or a glass-top table? Notice, next time, how special that glowing light makes the object it falls upon seem to be. Notice how important that shaft of light, or the shadows caused by light, become. And notice how your eye will follow that light or shadow and be distracted from other things in the room. The ray of sunlight that filters through a window or through a skylight can be controlled to some degree by manipulating a curtain or a shade, but natural light cannot be controlled in the way that we can make artificial light yield to our bidding. Light, then, is an important tool of camouflage, and in a dump camouflage is often the name of the game. Without light, of course, you can't see anything, a fact which, when it comes to certain aspects of dumps (the most obnoxious: cracked walls or whatever else you don't want seen), is an axiom well worth remembering. If there's an element of your dump that you don't want seen, don't light it. Instead, focus a spot of light on something else – a painting or a sculpture or a flower in a vase – anything, in short, that will distract the eye.

As to the means of lighting, rather than its functions, this is something that only you can teach yourself. Experiment and take a look at what light can do. Learn to "re-see." Look at what a light bulb does, what frosted or clear bulbs do to light and shadow, what tinted bulbs do to human moods. Look at what different types of lampshades do, the effects of shades that are opaque, the effects of shades that are not. And then research carefully the types of lighting fixtures that you want. Shop around and ask yourself the kinds of questions that you've learned to ask so well. Are those fancy track lights really worth the price, or can you achieve a similar result with inexpensive clip-on lamps? Must you have the table lamp you've set your heart on, or can you illuminate that corner of the room with a bare bulb behind a white silk umbrella? Is a new ceiling fixture absolutely necessary, or will a pleated wrapping-paper shade make the old one good as new? If necessity is in fact the mother of invention, then, when it comes to inexpensive lighting, experimentation is most certainly its father.

A dump for rent. Grab it—and make it your very own.

# Budgeting

DON'T WORRY ABOUT MONEY.

Sounds strange, doesn't it? Soothing, but a little off the wall. Who in this day and age can afford *not* to worry? Yet, when it comes to designing your space, money is only incidental.

As we've already seen, money can get in the way of the fundamental process of design – planning your ideal space. And since you already understand that your ideal is hardly going to be attained in the blinking of an eye, that it is going to be reached in stages over a period of time, why be concerned unduly with your cash flow? What a mistake it would be to tell yourself at the outset that you had only a set sum of money, say a thousand dollars, to work with. Then you'd automatically start by assigning small amounts of money to specific objects – $500 for sofa, $200 for a chair – rather than making long-range plans for a complete design that could begin with a few basics and be filled in by trading up over the years.

Mae West once said, "Keep a diary and someday it'll keep you. " Substitute "a ledger and some lists" for Mae's "diary," and you've encapsulated the primary message of this book. Keep refining the many lists that you make in planning your long-range design. Then arrange the items on your lists in chronological order – in the order in which you're going to have to lay out cash. Rugs before fabrics, fabrics before paints, and so on. This will become your "budget," and, if the total figure makes you turn pale, remember that it will not be spent all at once. If $500 for plaster and paint makes you blanch, remember that good materials may make the paint job last for five years, or sixty months, or for only a little over $4 a month, a bargain worth its weight in pleasure. This is exactly the sort of "positive" arithmetic you must do to deal realistically with your future expenses. As to the ledger, keep an accurate accounting of all your expenditures, down to the smallest nail. If you don't invest your hard-earned cash in junk, you should be able to sell all or most of your improvements to the next tenant when it comes time to move on to greener pastures. And you will.

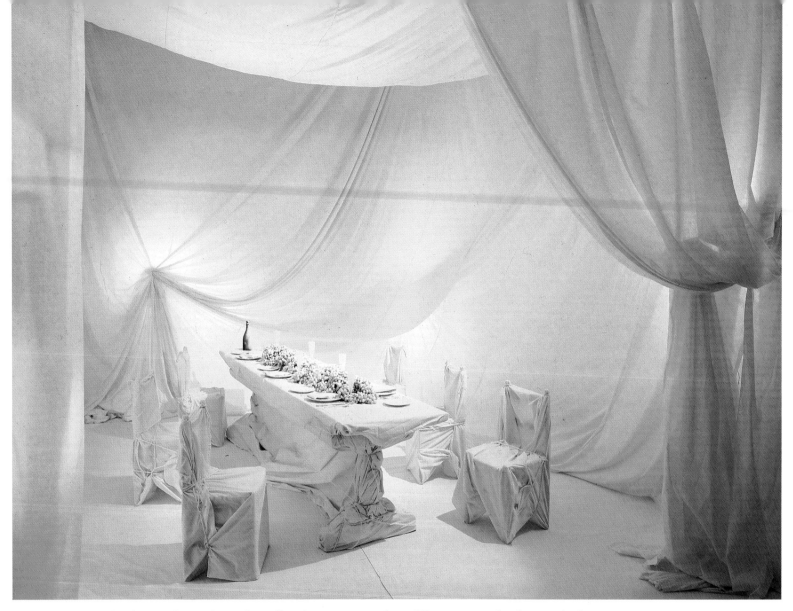

Muslin—300 yards of it—is obviously "such stuff as dreams are made on." By covering the floor with drop cloths and draping the walls and wrapping the furniture with cool, natural, billowing muslin, designer Antonio Morello and architect Donato Savoie have transformed this loft space into a dreamlike setting for a dinner party, to which, if it were only possible, Cocteau and Christo should be invited. By adapting this bold, dramatic idea on a smaller scale, you can turn your own space into a phantasmagoric tent, ending forever your battle with cracked and flaking walls.

# A GALLERY OF DREAM DUMPS

Since this book began with a dream, then it is only fitting that it should end with a dream. A gallery of dreams, in fact.

The spaces on the following pages represent a sort of summing up. They exemplify all the major principles of design that we've been discussing and represent a wide variety of types—from tenements to town houses, from lofts to modern lifeless cubes. All of them were dumps—until someone came along who recognized their possibilities and rescued them from decay and dissolution. By caring. By dreaming. By investing time, imagination, money, sweat, and love.

The places that follow are not necessarily better than other spaces previously shown. Nor are they the best nor the cream of the crop. They're simply more intense in one way or another. They all make ultimate statements, statements that reflect the personalities and even the innermost feelings of their designers. They represent the work of people who are totally involved with their environments. When you walk into each of these spaces, you have the feeling that the very air has been designed. For good design is far more than the mere arrangement of color, furniture, pictures, objects. It is a statement of self, something intangible, but a kind of magic, a kind of unseen, but deeply felt, energy. This is precisely why good design is so very difficult to catch on film. It is impossible to photograph the air, the ambience of a room.

What follows, then, is both promise and inspiration. The promise of what can be done with spaces that once were deemed to hold no promise at all. And the inspiration to screw up your courage, roll up your sleeves, open your wallet, and impose your personality on a dream of a dump.

*Opposite page:* The operative words here are "light," "color," "movement," "drama." Even though there is no way to photograph it adequately—you can't photograph "ambience"—this apartment seems to move to an unheard music. You almost want to snap your fingers and dance. Then you realize that to fully understand its statement, you'd have to fill it with lively people and photograph it with a motion picture camera.

To create an environment dramatically different from the world beyond his four walls, a space in sharp (almost shocking) contrast to the wreck of a tenement in which his apartment is contained, visual merchandiser/artist Peter Charbonneau designed this extraordinary "visual fantasy." A man who loves to entertain and who frequently gives large parties, Peter wanted a space that would come alive when there were people in it, a design that would transform his apartment into a stage on which his guests could interact. To achieve this end he required a strong background that would appear to change with the movement of people and with subtle changes in lighting, an aim achieved with the construction of angled wall partitions that not only hide the apartment's ugly, cracked walls, but give a sense of depth and greater space beyond. The dropped ceiling—rendered instantly theatrical by lighting mounted above it—is made from the plastic fabric used for automobile seat covers. Because the lucite table is seemingly "invisible," the room appears to be without furniture, an effect reinforced by the platforms that provide seating for party guests and also storage space. A deliberate study in contrasts, the modern mirrors stand in striking relief to the overmantel mirror of the 19th-century fireplace. The mantel itself holds models of Peter Charbonneau's displays currently in progress, where they can be "lived with" to measure their dramatic impact.

To say that this apartment makes a strong statement is understatement, to be sure. Its very boldness is certain to elicit either enthusiastic admiration or the standard "It's a nice place to visit, but. . . ." But what? The only meaningful "but" is that it doesn't make a bit of a difference whether you would want to live there or not. The apartment is a valid and exciting extension of its creator's personality. And it meets his needs and expectations. When it comes to good design, that is really all that matters.

The elegant studio apartment of interior designer Don Clay reflects his lifelong fascination with ecclesiastic architecture. A one-room space formed from the front parlor of a 19th-century town house, the apartment projects a clear, strong statement—a feeling of churchlike austerity that is saved from solemnity and made lively by its somewhat whimsical color scheme, fabrics, and textures. If one's first reaction is to sniff the air for the faint smell of incense, the sensation of "high seriousness" is cleverly abated by the unexpected shade of pink that predominates. If the space within a church soars heavenward, so does the space within Clay's room. Almost all the elements emphasize the height of the ceiling—the painted moldings, the almost Gothic paneling of the overmantel (pictured on this page), the mirrored doors to the kitchen (pictured on the right) and the en-

trance hall and the gold motifs on the headboard for the bed. So total is the designer's statement that, as in a church, he has almost enclosed himself in an environment that rejects the world outdoors. (Notice how the picture frame on the front door virtually denies any connection with the space beyond.) The beautiful headboard allows the bed to "float" within the room, where it serves not only as a large chaise, but as a divider that separates the sitting area from the dining area. As a solution to that most frequently encountered problem in one-room apartments—where to place a bed—it is intelligently conceived and merges superbly with the overall design.

Although my own apartment is a one-room studio, carved from an apartment twice its size some thirty or forty years ago, it is laid out in carefully defined areas that are evident both in the photograph above and in the floor plan on the opposite page. With its areas clearly delineated by use and not at all overlap-

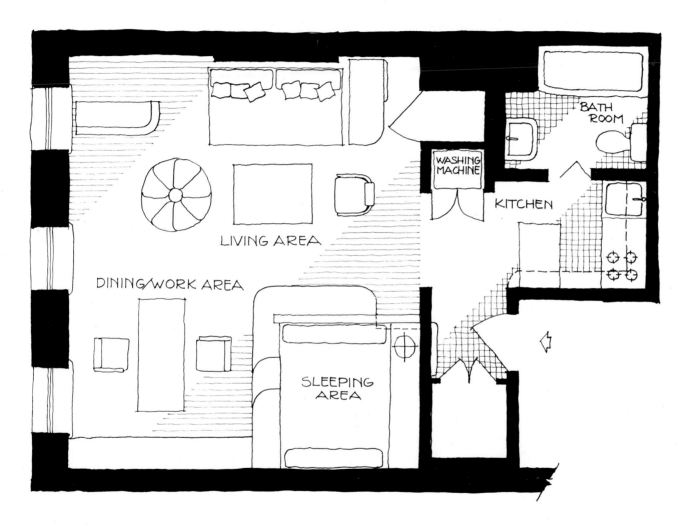

BATH ROOM

WASHING MACHINE

KITCHEN

LIVING AREA

DINING/WORK AREA

SLEEPING AREA

ping, the room functions as a small "house," complete with "upstairs" sleeping platform and "basement" storage space at the base of the sculptured platform. Another photograph of the apartment is shown on page 72. A plan for building the sofa on the left is given on page 74.

Until interior designer Juan Montoya applied his indelible magic touch to this unique apartment, it was just another unloved industrial space without a tenant along the docks of New York. Approached by the owner of the building and much taken with the space's handsome possibilities, Montoya accepted the challenge of designing it (on a very tight budget) as a "model apartment" for a future tenant. The result is a dream of good design, a room that takes full advantage of its unique view and massive space by remaining completely open in plan. Simply but tastefully furnished, the room provides all the amenities of comfortable living, but may be easily added to if the future tenant so desires. The only nightmare in this otherwise spectacular dream of urban paradise will be the window washer's bills.

*Overleaf, page 118*: If an apartment could wear a tuxedo, this would be it! But it would be a vintage tuxedo, one with the patina of age that gives it a timeless humanity as well as sharp, crisp formality. With bold grandeur and wit, designer/artist Carmelo Pomodoro has managed, simultaneously, to turn back the clock to his apartment's 19th-century origins and to keep it stylishly up-to-the-minute. With the exception of the original fireplace of the converted brownstone apartment, and the spectacular mahogany and oak flooring, discovered under layers of ancient linoleum, all of the handsome architectural flourishes—the fluted column, the framing of the overmantel mirror, the gilded valances above the windows—are the skillful additions of the designer. Far from diminishing the room, the intentionally black background provides a sense of infinity against which the antique elements and the modern happily coexist. The units of modular furniture, arranged on the bias, and covered with satin like the lapels of a formal tuxedo, bring the height of the ceiling—emphasized by the column—down to human scale. The bedroom *(page 119, left)*, a good example of the narrow, high-ceilinged room that comes from dividing a large space into smaller units, is nonetheless the dramatic counterpart to its adjoining living room. The interplay between vertical and horizontal elements, the almost outrageously large vase, the stylized classicism of the platform bed that repeats the fluting of the decorative column—all combine visually in an effect that is virtually surreal, a successful marriage between elegance and whimsy.

*Page 119, (right)*: To turn a modern box-like, lifeless space into a dream apartment is surely no mean feat, but it can be done with wit and imagination as the two remaining photographs on this page clearly show. (Another view of this unique apartment appears on page 120.) By treating the backgrounds of his apartment as if they were vast canvases upon which to create brilliant abstract paintings, an inventive designer has transformed an essentially commonplace interior into a vibrant fantasy. And his only expense was the paint necessary to make tangible the workings of his creative mind. Unlike the elaborately framed doorways in 19th-century buildings, modern doorways are frigid expanses of plaster, bare and raw. Here *(upper right)*, using pastel colors for his background and brilliantly-hued strips of fabric in the foreground, the designer has created a collage that effectively frames the doorway and suggests an approach to old-fashioned architectural ornamentation that is strictly 1980s. The forbidding modern kitchen *(below)* is considerably warmed by a creative use of paint, where standard metal wall cabinets, painted with a sponge, repeat the pattern of the enamel spongeware below.

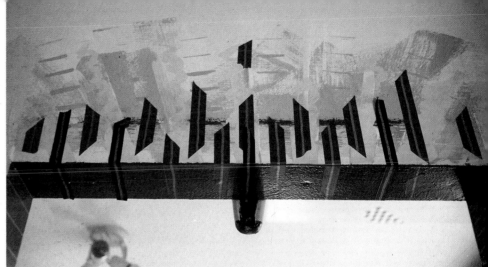

*Left:* The painterly abstractions of this window, through which the New York City skyline is viewed, suggest a clever updating of Piet Mondrian's visions of Manhattan painted more than forty years ago. The vibrant window treatment echoes the energy and vitality of the city beyond. Far from retreating from the rhythm of the city, this fanciful use of color and paint elects instead to celebrate it. *Opposite page:* The dreamlike bedroom of Leroy R. Boyack's San Francisco loft exemplifies the interior designer's aim "to create separate functional areas that would be consistent with a desire for unrestricted spaciousness." By dividing his large space with overlapping muslin panels that hang from ceiling to floor, and by creating an ever-changing interplay of light and shadow against the texture of the gently moving fabric, he attains a warm, personal atmosphere in a room without walls, a room that, like the kinetic sculpture to the right, is constantly in flux.

In the studio apartment of photographer Peter Vitale, the various functions of the single room are skillfully camouflaged to appear as a fully-integrated one-purpose living room, an effect so smoothly executed that one expects to find a bedroom and a dining room beyond the door. But the black throne-like sofa on a platform is, of course, a bed by night, while the table to the right doubles as a dining table and as a desk in close proximity to the reference shelves. Originally the rear parlor of a 19th-century town house that was the residence of a single family, the room retains its well-proportioned spaciousness and several of the architectural flourishes of its period. Yet its functional, but integrated, layout can be easily adapted to a room of any size. With its walls professionally painted and glazed, the room takes on additional depth, a refined "finished" quality that will last long enough to offset its cost.

Hiding a bed in a one-room apartment is perhaps the most common problem of studio living, and Peter Vitale's solution is both simple and practical. By placing a mattress on a black formica platform longer than the mattress, he effectively creates surfaces on both sides to serve as end tables by day and night stands by night. When it functions as a sofa, the mattress is covered with a simple fitted sheet fashioned from a flexible, but durable, fabric. Pillows of different textured materials complete the illusion of permanence, just as a full-length mirror appears to enlarge the handsome room.

The beautiful apartment illustrated on these two pages is dramatic evidence of what can happen to a dump over many years of attention and affection, tempered by restraint and patience and an understanding that an interior space, like its inhabitant, is ever-changing, always evolving, never finished. By continuously "trading up" over a long period of time, James Potucek, the designer of this apartment, amassed an eclectic collection of lovely objects, which, as they were added to the room one by one, slightly changed its character and forced the movement of furnishings from one place to another to achieve a proper "balance." Because the objects have been lovingly purchased over time with patient deliberateness, the room avoids the "decorator look" that is the antithesis of living design. (Those interested in inexpensive architectural effects should note how the gilded moldings and a painted pattern simulate an expensive frieze around the room.)

If, as Ecclesiastes says, "of the making of books there is no end," the same may be said of good interior design. There is no end to the inventiveness of creative people in adapting their environments to accommodate their needs and personalities, just as there is no end to the possibilities of transforming the most unpromising of spaces into places of great beauty and practical comfort.

In centuries past, American settlers who could afford neither costly architectural ornaments nor imported wall coverings realized that an inexpensive bucket of paint could perform wonders for the downcast soul. Rooms were painted, stenciled, or ornamented with architectural devices that were painted on the walls and ceilings. Interior walls, without enunciating it as such, were seen as vast canvases to be decorated by the creative imagination. In the 1930s, the great industrial designer Donald Deskey stenciled one wall of his 18th-century house with motifs adapted from his designs for the wall coverings of Radio City Music Hall. A few years later, in the 1940s, the sculptor/architect Frederick Kiesler created an elaborate modern fresco over the primitive pine mantel of a friend's early 19th-century rural cottage. Now, forty years later, Tom Simpson, a young New York artist, is decorating a tenement dump with little more than paint, personal vitality, and a prodigious talent. Like Alice through the looking glass, he is creating within a great unfinished canvas. It is a work in progress and indeed a dream.

# SOURCES AND SUPPLIERS

## Fabrics, Rugs, and Carpets

MATERIALS for furniture, draping, and covering walls and floors are not hard to find in any metropolitan area. Remnants shops and warehouse outlets are especially recommended as sources of inexpensive "leftovers." Discounted lines of fabric and carpeting can often be the most imaginative quality materials available to the public. Their lack of commercial appeal may recommend them highly. Listed are outlets offering various types of current and discontinued lines. The stock, of course, is constantly changing.

B & J Fabrics
263 W. 40th St.
New York, NY 10018
(212) 221-9287

S. Beckenstein, Inc.
(Fabrics)
130 Orchard St.
New York, NY 10002
(212) 475-4525

Carpet Forest
3115 Irving Park Rd.
Chicago, IL 60618
(312) 478-9560
also at 4803 N. Milwaukee,
   Chicago

End of the Roll Carpets
2010 University Blvd.
Adelphi, MD 20783
(301) 434-3553

Fabric Barn
2717 N. Clark
Chicago, IL 60614
(312) 477-5000

Fabric Scouts
818 Lexington Ave.
New York, NY 10021
(212) 391-2630

Fabric Showroom
319 Washington
Brighton, MA 02135
(617) 783-4343

Fabrications
114 Newbury St.
Boston, MA 02116
(617) 267-3529
also at Brookline, Cambridge,
   and Newton

Floor World Warehouse
272 Bethlehem Pike, Rte. 309
Colmar, PA 18915
(215) 822-0181

OK Furniture Carpet
   Liquidators
1475 Flatbush Ave.
Brooklyn, NY 11210
(212) 859-8995

P & S Fabrics
923 Arch St.
Philadelphia, PA 19104
(215) 922-5261

Philadelphia Flooring
116 N. 2nd St.
Philadelphia, PA 19106
(215) 627-2843

Ronald's Fabrics
1946 Chestnut St.
Philadelphia, PA 19104
(215) 386-2587

Silk Surplus
818 Lexington Ave.
New York, NY 10021
also at Paramus and Westbury

Terminal Fabric Warehouse
6999 N.E. 2nd Ave.
Miami, FL 33138
also at Carol City and S. Miami

## Furniture

WHEN FRIENDS and relatives have nothing more to give, the Salvation Army and Goodwill appear to have run out of supplies, and the pickings along the street on trash day have turned slim — it is time to turn to the retail marketplace. This is not as dire an alternative as it may seem at first. For many years, decorators of dumps have turned to unpainted furniture suppliers, butcher-block purveyors, and with-it contemporary furniture dealers such as Workbench, Door Store, HomePlace, Scandinavian Design, and Furniture-in-the-Raw for hard-to-find, reasonably-priced items. It hurts to have to pay a cent for a new table or chair, but there *are* manufacturers and retailers who share your appreciation for value, style, and utility. Many specialize in multipurpose objects suitable for small apartments. Manufacturers who offer their work to the public are indicated by the letter (M); all other listings are for retail outlets.

Abacus Plastics (M)
135 W. 26th St.
New York, NY 10001
(212) 807-7966

AMCO Corp. (M)
901 N. Kilpatrick Ave.
Chicago, IL 60651
(312) 379-2100

Amstore Movable Wall Systems
104 E. 40th St.
New York, NY 10016
(212) 490-1255

Andre Furniture Industries (M)
125 Edwin Rd.
S. Windsor, CT 06074
(203) 528-8826

Apartment Stuff
Charter Oak Mall
940 Silver Ln.
E. Hartford, CT 06108
(203) 569-3256

Arise Futon Mattress Co. (M)
37 Wooster St.
New York, NY 10013
(212) 925-0310

Au Naturel
2759 S.W. 27th Ave.
Miami, FL 33133
(305) 856-3399

Bare Old Necessities
210 Fifth St.
W. Des Moines, IA 50321
(515) 255-3330

The Bare Woods
4678 Alvarado Canyon Rd.
San Diego, CA 92120
(619) 280-5350

Barn Furniture Outlet
outlets in Los Angeles, Glendale,
  and Van Nuys
Call (213) 240-4035 for informa-
tion

Bedworks (M)
121 W. 19th St.
New York, NY 10011
(212) 777-5640

Bon Marche
74 Fifth Ave.
New York, NY 10011
(212) 620-5550
also at 1060 Third Ave., New
  York

The Boston Bedroom
Rte. 9
Brookline, MA 02147
(617) 731-6038

J & D Brauner
298 Bowery
New York, NY 10012
(212) 477-2830

Butcher Block & More
1600 S. Clinton
Chicago, IL 60616
(312) 421-1138
also at Downers Grove and
  Glenview

Butcher Block Store
511 Queen St. W.
Toronto, Ontario
Canada
(416) 746-3633

The Children's Room
318 E. 45th St.
New York, NY 10017
(212) 687-3868

CiBon Interiors
526 N. Cassingham Rd.
Bexley, OH 43209
(614) 253-6555

Conran's (mail order)
145 Huguenot St.
New Rochelle, NY 10801
(914) 632-0515

Conran's (retail)
The Market at Citicorp
160 E. 54th St.
New York, NY 10022
(212) 371-2225
also at 2-8 Astor Pl., New York,
  NY; New Rochelle, NY;
  Washington, DC; Fairfax,
  VA; Hackensack, NJ;
  Manhasset, NY, King of
  Prussia, PA

Contemporary Comfort
5127 E. Colfax
Denver, CO 80204
(303) 333-1776
also at Fort Collins, North
   Glenn, Colorado Springs,
   Boulder, Lakewood

Contemporary Galleries
221 W. 4th
Cincinnati, Oh 45202
(513) 621-3113

Copenhagen Imports
121 W. Main St.
Moorestown, NJ 08057
(609) 235-9243
also at Woodbury

Country Workshop (M)
95 Rome St.
Newark, NJ 07105
(201) 589-3407

Creative Comfort
130 Brighton St.
Boston, MA 02169
(617) 369-7173

Custom Art Furniture (M)
225 E. 24th St.
New York, NY 10010
(212) 369-1191

Danco
269 Locust St.
Northampton, MA 01060
(413) 586-3620
also in Hatfield

Decorators Warehouse
2030 S. 30th Ave.
Hallandale, FL 33009
(305) 454-1117

Decorators Warehouse
665 11th Ave.
New York, NY 10019
(212) 757-1106

Design Furniture Warehouse
902 Broadway
New York, NY 10010
(212) 673-8900

Design Union
1330 Old River Rd.
Cleveland, OH 44113
(216) 621-2002

Designs in Shelving
420 S. 5th St.
Camden, NJ 08103
(609) 966-0170

Dixie Foam
(Foam Mattresses)
20 East 20th St.
New York, NY 10003
(212) 777-3626

Domicil
1520 Blvd. LaBelle
Laval, Quebec
Canada
(514) 688-2270

Domus
471 Boston Post Rd.
Orange, CT 06477
(203) 795-0277
also at Farmington

Door Store
1 Park Ave.
New York, NY 10016
(212) 679-9700
also at White Plains, Ithaca

Door Store
3140 M St., NW
Washington, D.C.
(202) 333-7737
also outlets throughout DC area;
   Richmond, VA; Florida; and
   Texas

Fastman's Unpainted Furniture
16 E. Baltimore Pike
Clifton Heights, PA 19018
(215) 623-2951

Functional Furnishing
601 N. High St.
Columbus, OH 43215
(614) 228-3463

The Furniture Factory
2531 N. Clark St.
Chicago, IL 60614
(312) 248-0540
also at Oak Park and Wilmette

Furniture-in-the-Raw
1021 Second Ave.
New York, NY 10022
(212) 355-7373

The Golden Nagas
3103 Geary Blvd.
San Francisco, CA 94118
(415) 752-7693

Gothic Cabinet Craft
(15 stores in NY area)
Call (212) 729-2159 for informa-
tion

Gothic Craft
2655 N. Clark St.
Chicago, IL 60614
(312) 248-5551
also at 4862 W. Irving Park Rd.,
    Chicago, and 933 W. Bel-
    mont, Chicago

Habitare
3412 Poplar Ave.
Memphis, TN 38116
(901) 458-1260

The Happy Viking
Rte. 309
Hatfield, PA 19440
(215) 362-1900
also at Wilmington, DE

Harbor Design
63 Long Wharf
Boston, MA 02110
(617) 227-3349

HomePlace
4025 Goldfinch St.
San Diego, CA 92103
(619) 297-5201
also at La Jolla

Hoot Judkins
1142 Sutter
San Francisco, CA 94109
(415) 673-5454
also at Santa Clara and Millbrae

Horizon
8600 W. Pico Blvd.
Los Angeles, CA 90035
(213) 652-4933

House of Denmark
10611 W. 63rd St.
Kansas City, MO 64113
(913) 268-6626

Howard Hill
Airport Circle
Pennsauken, NJ 08110
(609) 663-0560

Interior Systems
Monroeville Mall
Monroeville, PA
(412) 372-6622

International Design Center
100 Second Ave., N.
Minneapolis, MN 55401
(612) 341-3441

Jakanna Woodworks
122011 Nebel St.
Rockville, MD 20852
(301) 770-9663

Jensen-Lewis (M)
89 Seventh Ave.
New York, NY 10011
(212) 929-4880

Limitless Design Corp.
26 Otis St.
Cambridge, MA 02139
(617) 354-1292

The Loft Bed Store
611 Hungerford
Rockville, MD 20850
(301) 340-0998
also at Alexandria, VA

Luminaire
16 Miracle Mile
Coral Gables, FL 33134
(305) 448-7367
alto at Plantation

Mazza Frame and Furniture (M)
35-10 10th St.
Long Island City, NY 11106
(212) 721-9287

Mobilia
65 Geary Blvd.
San Francisco, CA 94108
(415) 982-9911
also at Palo Alto, Berkeley,
    Walnut Creek, Novato, Santa
    Clara

Modern Furniture Manufactur-
    ing (M)
1421 N.E. 129th St.
N. Miami, FL 33161
(305) 625-4033

Murphy Door Bed Co. (M)
40 E. 34th St.
New York, NY 10016
(212) 682-8936

Naked Furniture
806 N. Clark St.
Chicago, IL 60643
(312) 337-7344
also at Des Plaines, Schaumburg,
    Wheaton, Downers Grove,
    Naperville

Oddities
5415 Walnut St.
Pittsburgh, PA 15232
(412) 687-3921

Rennert Moving Mats
93 Greene St.
New York, NY 10012
(212) 925-1463

Room Plus Furniture
1555 Third Ave.
New York, NY 10028
(212) 410-9393

Roxy Modern Furniture
115 W. 23rd St.
New York, NY 10011
(212) 675-1827

Saah Bookcase
2330 Columbia Pike
Arlington, VA 22204
(703) 920-1500
also at Marlow Heights, Wood-
    bridge

Scan Contemporary Furnishings
404 Reisterstown Rd.
Pikeville, MD 21208
(301) 486-2500
also at Georgetown, Falls
    Church, Takoma Park,
    Wheaton, Columbia

Scandia House
1733 Chestnut St.
Philadelphia, PA 19103
(215) 563-0842

Scandinavian Design
920 N. Michigan Ave.
Chicago, IL 60611
(312) 664-9232

also at 548 W. Diversey Pkwy.,
Chicago; Evanston;
Northbrook; Schaumburg;
Oak Brook; Lombard;
Aurora; Orland Park;
Matheson; Waukegan

Shelves & Cabinets Unlimited
4750 Kearny Mesa Rd.
San Diego, CA 92111
(619) 578-4200

also at Del Mar

Shilling
25 Mt. Auburn St.
Cambridge, MA 02139
(617) 661-0375

SofaBed Warehouse
940 Battery St.
San Francisco, CA 94111
(415) 397-1550

also at Santa Clara and Pleasant
Hill

Space Beds
1564 Bush St.
San Francisco, CA 94109
(415) 474-4160

Space Makers for Living (M)
33 W. 21st St.
New York, NY 10010
(212) 242-6619

Storehouse
Atlanta, GA
call (404) 261-3482 for informa-
tion
also at Lenox Sq., Northlake II;
Buckhead; Sandy Springs

Storehouse
4105 Hillsboro Rd.
Nashville, TN 37215
(615) 385-0812

Storehouse
1532 St. Charles Ave.
New Orleans, LA 70130
(504) 524-9771

also at 3750 Veterans Blvd.,
New Orleans

Tempus
555 Steeprock Dr.
Toronto, Ont.
Canada
(416) 635-6999

This End Up Furniture Co.
1139 Second Ave.
New York, NY 10022
(212) 755-6065

also at 461 W. Broadway, New
York; White Plains; Paramus;
Wayne; Woodbridge;
Lawrenceville

Unpainted Furniture Center
3526 Jackson Ave.
Memphis, TN 38122
(901) 458-3341

Upstairs/Downstairs
1701 Post Rd.
Westport, CT 06880
(203) 255-6136

Warehouse Imports
3901 Main St.
Manayunk, PA 19127
(215) 482-8000

Wall Units Inc.
12211 Santa Monica Blvd.
W. Los Angeles, CA 90025
(213) 826-8379

also at San Diego, Long Beach,
San Fernando Valley, Orange
County

Wood Market
234 Dominion Rd., NE
Vienna, VA 22180
(703) 281-6300

Workbench
270 Park Ave. S.
New York, NY 10016
(212) 532-7900
also at 1320 Third Ave. and
    2091 Broadway, New York;

Brooklyn; Manhasset; Lake
Grove; Scarsdale; Albany;
Hackensack; Princeton;
Westport; Hartford;
Philadelphia; Cambridge

## Lighting

SOMEONE should open a chain of discount lighting outlets. Depression sets in when you encounter the usual sea of showroom swag lamps and phony Tiffany-like baubles. But persist. You can probably find what you want in the glare of the lights. Look for the marked-down items, the simply designed fixtures that don't twinkle on and off, bubble up, or hit you in the eye. New York City is the center of contemporary lighting manufacture in America, and you are likely to find many more bargains in the Big Apple than elsewhere—if you can swing a trip.

Bowery Lighting Corp.
132 Bowery
New York, NY 10013
(212) 966-2485

Capital Lighting & Supply
3950 Wheeler Ave.
Alexandria, VA 22304
(703) 623-6000

Harem Lites
139 Bowery
New York, NY 10002
(212) 226-3042

The Light Switch
2110 N.E. 123rd St.
N. Miami, FL 33161
(305) 895-0264

Lighting Center Ltd.
1097 Second Ave.
New York, NY 10022
(212) 758-1562

Jo Skymer Lamps
U.S. 130 and Garden Ave.
Pennsauken, NJ 08110
(609) 662-2666

Thrift House
4 Delancey St.
New York, NY 10002
(212) 505-0300

Universal Electric Discount
  Outlet
3124 Dundas St. W.
Toronto, Ontario
Canada
(416) 767-5454

Warehouse of Lights
4398 S.W. 74th Ave.
Miami, FL 33155
(305) 266-3460

---

## Designers Whose Work Appears in This Book

Philip Almeida
(Interior Designer)
128 W. 71st St.
New York, NY 10023
(212) 362-6143

Bruce Bierman
(Interior Designer)
29 W. 15th St.
New York, NY 10011
(212) 243-1935

Leonard Braunschweiger
(Architectural Designer)
699 Madison Ave.
New York, NY 10021
(212) 355-6675

Leroy R. Boyack
(Interior Designer)
59 Rogers St.
San Francisco, CA 94103
(415) 626-7785

Don Clay Studio
(Interior Designer)
34 W. 10th St.
New York, NY 10011
(212) 228-9533

Thom Deligter Interior Design
212 W. 71st St.
New York, NY 10023
(212) 580-1824

Peter Fasano
(Painter of Floorcloths and
    Fabrics)
1309 Madison Ave.
New York, NY 10028
(212) 534-8799

Dane Goodman
P.O. Box 3880
Santa Barbara, CA 93105
(805) 965-2134

Mel Hammock
(Interior Designer/Stylist)
405 E. 54th St.
New York, NY 10022
(212) 759-9209

David Hecht
(Interior Designer)
43-08 41st St.
Sunnyside, NY 11104
(212) 784-0958

Juan Montoya
(Interior Designer)
80 Eighth Ave.
New York, NY 10011
(212) 242-3622

P.D.J. Design
(Nicholas Politis and Richard
    Des Jardins)
525 West End Ave.
New York, NY 10024
(212) 580-9540

Carmelo Pomodoro
(Designer)
111 E. 36th St.
New York, NY 10016
(212) 532-7287

Corbett Reynolds
(Fabric/Wallcovering Designer)
1153 Neil Ave.
Columbus, OH 43201
(614) 294-8309

Thomas H. Simpson
(Artist/Environmental Designer)
17 Dorian Lane
Rochester, NY 14626

Studio Morsa
(Antonio Morello and Donato
    Savoie)
247 Centre St.
New York, NY 10013
(212) 226-4324

Halsted Welles Associates, Inc.
(Landscape Architects)
287 E. Houston St.
New York, NY 10002
(212) 777-5440

# Acknowledgments

B Y ITS VERY NATURE, an illustrated book is a collaborative effort. As interesting as my ideas on decorating might be, they would be rendered meaningless without specific illustrations to illuminate my points of view. In writing this book, I have been fortunate to have the enthusiastic assistance of designers and photographers whose suggestions and photographs have helped to shape its content. These talented people are all listed in the credits that follow, and I am pleased to acknowledge their generous contributions.

In addition to these colleagues, I am especially indebted to Jim Brinkley for his patient help in keeping the train on the track during a sometimes hazardous journey; Richard Des Jardins for helping to unleash that nebulous quality within me called "intuition"; Ray Kohn for inspiring me to learn about the possibilities of inventiveness through his personal example; and my editor, Martin Greif, for allowing me to talk about design in my own voice without having to pretend that it is somehow a cosmic mystery to be understood by only the chosen few.

# Credits

Frontispiece, p. 2 — Private collection
p. 12 — The Bettmann Archives
p. 14 — Private collection
p. 15 — Courtesy of Helen J. Kelly

p. 16 — Courtesy of Nicholas Politis
p. 17 — Courtesy of Christopher Varga
p. 18 — Emiko Nagashima
pp. 22-23 — Photographs courtesy of Edward Oleksak

p. 24—Peter M. Fine
p. 27—Courtesy of Richard Des Jardins
p. 29—Courtesy of Nicholas Politis
p. 31—Peter M. Fine
p. 32—Courtesy of Nicholas Polites
p. 33—Richard Champion
p. 35—Jaime Ardiles-Arce
p. 36—Peter M. Fine
pp. 38-39—© Paul Warchol/ESTO
p. 40—Courtesy of Peter Vitale
p. 42—Bruce Wolf
p. 44—Emiko Nagashima
p. 46—Courtesy of Halsted Welles
pp. 47-49—Emiko Nagashima
p. 50—Courtesy of Christopher Varga
p. 52—Courtesy of David Hecht
p. 54—Courtesy of Nicholas Politis
p. 56—Courtesy of Juan Montoya
p. 62—Richard Champion
p. 64 (left)—Courtesy of Nicholas Politis
p. 64 (right)—Richard Champion
p. 66—Emiko Nagashima
p. 68—Courtesy of Peter Vitale
p. 69—Courtesy of Nicholas Politis
pp. 70-71—Peter M. Fine
p. 72—Lynn Karlin
p. 74—Emiko Nagashima
p. 76—Peter M. Fine
pp. 78-80—Courtesy of Professor Julius Panero,
Fashion Institute of Technology

pp. 81-82—Courtesy of David Hecht
p. 84—Emiko Nagashima
p. 86 (left)—Emiko Nagashima
p. 86 (right)—Richard Champion
p. 87—Richard Champion
p. 88—Courtesy of Thom Deligter Interior Design
p. 94—Courtesy of Nicholas Politis
p. 98—Photograph courtesy of Edward Oleksak;
photograph by Adam Titone
p. 100—Emiko Nagashima
p. 102—Courtesy of Peter Charbonneau
p. 104—Peter M. Fine
p. 106—The New York Public Library Picture
Collection
p. 108—© Peter Aaron/ESTO
p. 110—Ensminger © 1980
pp. 112-13—Elizabeth Heyert
p. 114—Lynn Karlin
p. 115—Emiko Nagashima
p. 116—Jaime Ardiles-Arce
pp. 118-19 (left)—Courtesy of Peter Vitale
p. 119 (top and bottom, right)—Photographs by
Joshua Greene
p. 120—Joshua Greene
p. 121—Mary E. Nichols
pp. 122, 124-25—Courtesy of Peter Vitale
p. 126—Peter M. Fine

# INDEX